HIGH ON...
EXHIBITION DESIGN

HIGH ON...

EXHIBITION DESIGN

CURATED BY RALF DAAB

Editorial project:
2021 © **booq** publishing, S.L.
c/ Domènech, 7-9, 2º 1ª
08012 Barcelona, Spain
T: +34 93 268 80 88
www.booqpublishing.com

ISBN 978-84-9936-698-2

Curator:
Ralf Daab
© HIGH ON... by Ralf Daab

Editorial coordinator and layout:
Claudia Martínez Alonso

Art director:
Mireia Casanovas Soley

Translation:
booq publishing, S.L.

Translation introduction:
Gérard A. Goodrow

Printing in Spain

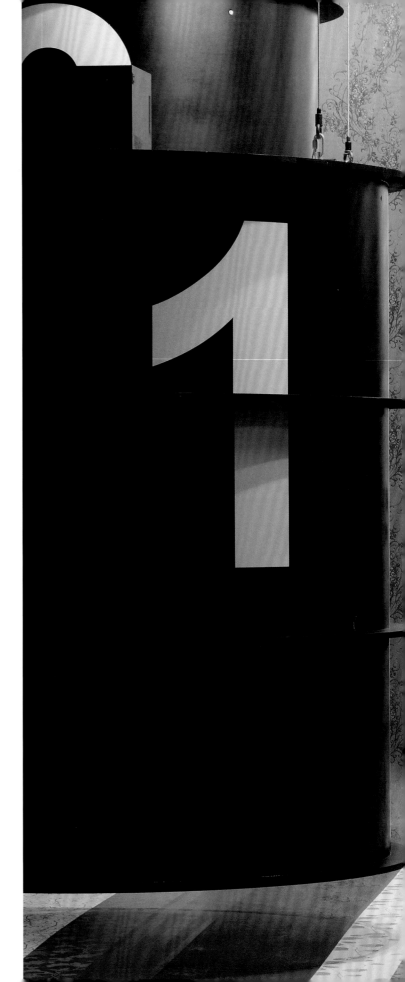

14

EINLEITUNG
INTRODUCTION

18

ATELIER BRÜCKNER

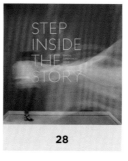

28

ATELIER MARKGRAPH

38

BRANDHERM + KRUMREY

48

CBA LEMENS BACHMANN
ARCHITEKTEN

58

COPYRIGHT COMMUNICATIONS

68

DAYDREAMERS DESIGN

78

DESIGNBÜRO FÖN, DESIGN_

88

FUHRIMANN HÄCHLER
ARCHITEKTEN /
LAUFEN BATHROOMS AG

98

GIGLER HOLZ-DESIGN

108

JOCHEN HUNGER MUSEUM &
EXHIBITION DESIGN

118

JÜRGENSARCHITEKTEN

128

KAUFFMANN THEILIG & PARTNER

138

MAIER + HOLLENBECK ARCHITEKTEN

148

PRINZTRÄGER

158

QUADT INTERIOR ARCHITECTURE

168

RANGER DESIGN

178

RAUMKONTOR INNENARCHITEKTUR

188

SONS. AGENTUR FÜR STRATEGISCHE UND KREATIVE MARKENENTWICKLUNG

198

STUDIO LAKRITS

208

STUDIO SASCH

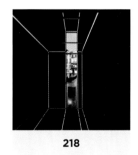

218

UEBERHOLZ

228

VERZEICHNIS
DIRECTORY

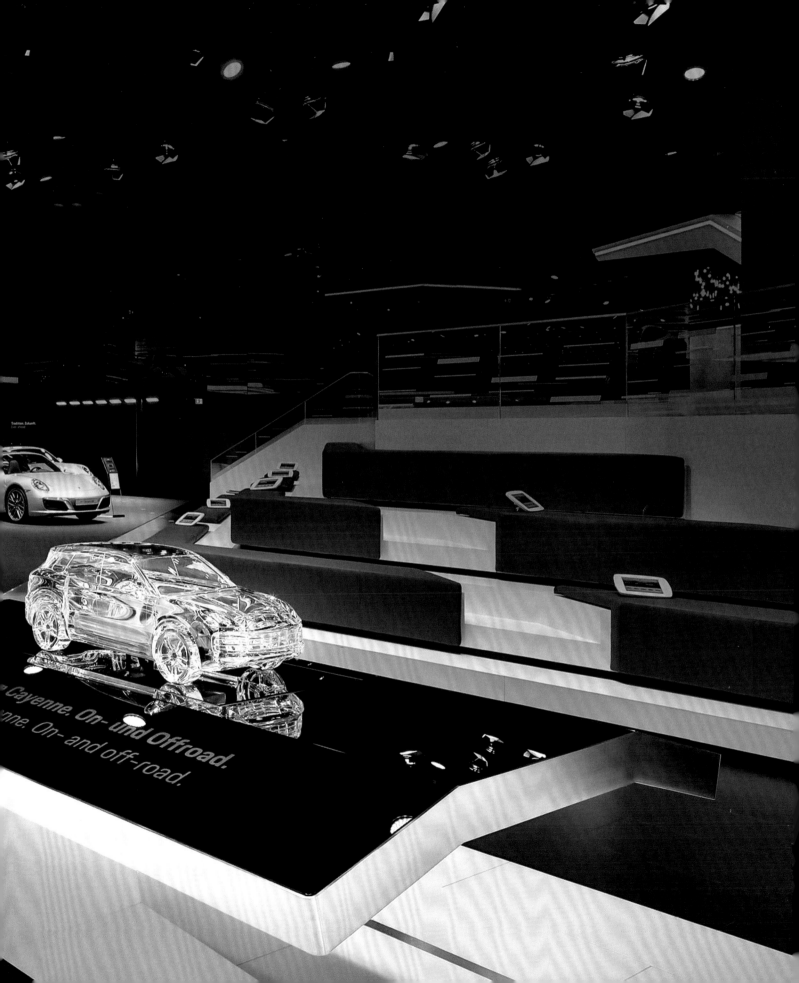

Ob Ausstellungen, Messestände, Markenwelten, Museen oder Showrooms, die Inszenierungen von Firmen, Marken, Produkten und Themen bedingen einer engen Zusammenarbeit verschiedener Disziplinen.

Von der Idee über die Konzeption, die Architektur, die Szenografie, das Grafikdesign, das Produktdesign und das Mediendesign entstehen analoge und digitale Räume, die Emotionen bei Kunden, beim Publikum und bei den Besuchern hervorrufen, die ein nachhaltiges Erlebnis und damit eine Verbundenheit erzeugen. Dies können dauerhafte oder temporäre Präsentationen sein.

Die in diesem Buch vorgestellten, vielfach mit nationalen und internationalen Preisen ausgezeichneten Projekte, zeigen eindrucksvolle Interpretationen unterschiedlicher Thematiken.

Ralf Daab

VAL
DESIGN BY KONSTANTIN GRCIC

INO
DESIGN BY TOAN NGUYEN

Whether exhibitions, trade fair stands, brand worlds, museums, or showrooms, the staging of companies, brands, products, and topics require close cooperation between various disciplines.

From the idea to the conception, the architecture, the scenography, the graphic design, the product and media design, analog and digital spaces are created that evoke emotions in customers, the audience, and visitors, creating a lasting experience and thus a bond. These can be permanent or temporary presentations.

The projects presented in this book, which have received numerous national and international awards, show impressive interpretations of various topics.

Ralf Daab

ATELIER BRÜCKNER

Partner: René Walkenhorst, Britta Nagel, Shirin Frangoul-Brückner, Prof. Eberhard Schlag. Assoziierte Partner (stehend): Cord-Hinrich Grote, Kathrin Milic-Grunwald, Bernd Möller, Michel Casertano, Stefanie Klinge, Jana Fröhlich, Tanja Zöllner, Marco Müller, Dominik Hegemann

ATELIER BRÜCKNER konzipiert und gestaltet Ausstellungen und Architekturen; seit 1997 entstehen Szenografien, die im internationalen Kontext Maßstäbe setzen. Szenografisch bauen heißt Architekturen entwickeln, die – ob temporär oder dauerhaft – von der Gestaltung der Hülle über den Entwurf der Innenräume bis hin zur Wahl der Materialien, aus dem zu vermittelnden Inhalt heraus erdacht sind. Raum, Grafik, Licht, Ton und digitale Medien bringen die Inhalte zum Ausdruck. Es entstehen Erlebnisräume, die Geschichten erzählen und Wissen vermitteln. Interaktion führt zu einer längeren Verweildauer und zur Identifikation mit den Inhalten. Mit 120 Mitarbeitern – verteilt auf die Standorte Stuttgart und Seoul – zählt ATELIER BRÜCKNER zu den führenden Szenografen weltweit. Schwerpunkt sind Projekte für Museen und Marken. Konzeption, Planung und Umsetzung kommen aus einer Hand.

ATELIER BRÜCKNER conceives and designs exhibitions and architectures; since 1997 it has been creating scenographies that set standards in an international context. Scenographic building means developing architectures that, whether temporary or permanent, are conceived from the content to be conveyed, from the design of the shell to the design of the interior spaces and the choice of materials. Space, graphics, light, sound and digital media express the content. Experiential spaces are created that tell stories and convey knowledge. Interaction leads to a longer stay and identification with the content. With 120 employees, distributed between the Stuttgart and Seoul locations, ATELIER BRÜCKNER is one of the leading scenographers worldwide. The focus is on projects for museums and brands. Conception, planning and implementation come from a single source.

HERGESTELLT IN DER SCHWEIZ
MADE IN SWITZERLAND

LINDT HOME OF CHOCOLATE, KILCHBERG, SCHWEIZ

Es duftet nach Schokolade! Die Chocolate Tour im Lindt Home of Chocolate vermittelt Ursprung, Geschichte und Produktion der zartschmelzenden Delikatesse. Sie stellt Schweizer Spezifika heraus und macht das kakaohaltige Produkt auf 1500 Quadratmetern Ausstellungstellungsfläche mit allen Sinnen erlebbar. Die Museumsausstellung befindet sich in einem Neubau der Schweizer Architekten Christ & Gantenbein am Hauptsitz von Lindt & Sprüngli in Kilchberg bei Zürich. Den Auftakt der Schokoladenwelt bildet im Foyer des Museums der weltweit höchste, freistehende Schokoladenbrunnen. Getragen vom Duft der Schokolade begeben sich die Besucher auf Entdeckungstour. Klänge, Gerüche, Medien- und Mitmachstationen lassen sie Teil unterschiedlicher Szenerien werden. Jeder Ausstellungsraum ist individuell gestaltet und vermittelt sinnlich wie informativ einen Aspekt der Schokoladenwelt.

LINDT HOME OF CHOCOLATE, KILCHBERG, SWITZERLAND

It smells like chocolate! The Chocolate Tour in the Lindt Home of Chocolate conveys the origins, history and production of the melt-in-the-mouth delicacy. It highlights Swiss specifics and enables the cocoa-containing product to be experienced with all the senses on an exhibition space of 1,500 square meters. The museum exhibition is located in a new building designed by the Swiss architects Christ & Gantenbein at Lindt & Sprüngli's headquarters in Kilchberg near Zurich. The world of chocolate starts with the world's tallest, free-standing chocolate fountain in the foyer of the museum. Carried by the scent of chocolate, visitors embark on a tour of discovery. Sounds, smells, media and hands-on stations make them part of different scenarios. Each exhibition room is individually designed and conveys an aspect from the world of chocolate in a sensual and informative way.

INNOVATION
LAB

WILLKOMMEN IN DER ZUKUNFT. Hier beschäftigen wir uns mit den vielfältigen Fragen von morgen – technisch, gesellschaftlich und ökologisch. Das Herzstück des Innovation Lab ist die moderne Pilotanlage. Auf ihr entwickeln Spezialisten die neusten Schokoladenkreationen. Aber wir denken weiter: Welche globalen Themen beeinflussen die Schokoladenindustrie? Welche Innovationen führten damals zu den Produkten und Verfahren, die heute Klassiker sind? Wie können wir sie weiterentwickeln, und wo ist unsere Innovationskraft gefragt? Wir haben inspirierende und überraschende Antworten für Sie – und eine Menge Fragen.

WELCOME TO THE FUTURE. This is where we tackle the manifold questions of tomorrow – from a technical, social and ecological perspective. The modern pilot plant is at the heart of the Innovation Lab. There, experts and specialists develop the latest chocolate creations. But we also like to think ahead: Which global issues influence the chocolate industry? Which innovations have led us to the products and processes that are classics today? How can we develop these further, and where is our power of innovation really needed? We have some inspiring and surprising answers for you, as well as plenty of questions.

LIMESMUSEUM AALEN

Rund fünf Kilometer südlich der antiken Limes-Linie, am Standort des Römerkastells Ala II Flavia, liegt das größte Römermuseum Süddeutschlands: Das Limesmuseum Aalen. Es bietet Besuchern zwei Zugänge zur Antike: Im abgedunkelt inszenierten Erdgeschoss tauchen sie in die Lebenswelt der Römer und Germanen ein. Großformatige Illustrationen prägen die Raumbilder der einzelnen Lebensbereiche. Antike Personen erzählen aus ihrem Leben. Sie sind in Form von Cut-Outs präsent. Im lichtdurchfluteten Obergeschoss geht es um die Erforschung der ehemaligen Grenzlinie. Es entsteht eine zusammenhängende Übersicht der antiken Limes-Orte im heutigen Baden-Württemberg. Ihnen sind bedeutende archäologische Funde zugeordnet. Das Raumbild erinnert an ein Labor. Beide Etagen haben Querverweise zur Grabungslandschaft, die das Museum umgibt. Die Ausstellung beleuchtet den Limes als Synonym einer historischen Grenze und hinterfragt die Funktion und Bedeutung von Grenzbauten in Vergangenheit und Gegenwart.

LIMES MUSEUM AALEN

Around five kilometres to the south of the ancient Limes line, on the site of the Roman castle Ala II Flavia, lies the largest Roman museum in Southern Germany: the Limes Museum Aalen. Visitors are offered two approaches to antiquity: in the darkened setting created on the ground floor, they are submersed in the living environment of the Romans and Teutons. Large-scale illustrations characterize different spatial images of the individual areas of life. Ancient people tell about their everyday lives. They are presented as silhouettes in the room. Flooded with light, the upper storey is all about research into the former border. A connected overview of the ancient Limes sites in today's Baden-Wurttemberg is created. The objects on display are aligned with the location of the respective find. The spatial image is reminiscent of a laboratory. Both floors have cross-references to the excavation site that surrounds the museum. The exhibition focuses on the Limes as a synonym for a historical boundary and questions the function and importance of boundaries in the past and at present.

HYUNDAI – DESIGN YOUR OWN WORLD, LAS VEGAS, USA

Mobilität der Zukunft: Mit dem Messestand „Design your own world" präsentiert Hyundai seine Vision des autonomen Fahrens. Abgeschottet vom Trubel der Messe ziehen sechs kugelförmige Glaskokons die Aufmerksamkeit auf sich. Die umgebende 360-Grad-Leinwand erweckt den Eindruck als bewegten sie sich durch eine futuristische Stadt. Ihre Ausstattung passen die Kokons dem Bedarf der Passagiere an: Begleitet von der K.I. Maia entdecken die Besucher vier Mustermodi die es erlauben, während der Fahrt Sport zu treiben, sich weiterzubilden, zu arbeiten oder per Drohne vom Auto aus einzukaufen. Die Fahrtzeit wird zu wertvoller Freizeit. Im ersten Modus, der Sports Experience, bestreiten die Passagiere beispielsweise einen sportlichen Wettkampf. Ausfahrbare Griffe dienen als Ruder; die bespielbare Frontscheibe der Kokons zeigt den Fortschritt im Rennen an. Im zweiten Modus, der Discovery Experience, entdecken die Passagiere die Weiten unserer Galaxie und können ihr neu erworbenes Wissen in einem Quiz testen. Die Besucher werden aktiv einbezogen und erleben, wie sie ihre Reisezeit effektiv und spielerisch nutzen können.

HYUNDAI – DESIGN YOUR OWN WORLD, LAS VEGAS, USA

Mobility of the future: With the "Design your own world" exhibition stand at CES in Las Vegas, Hyundai presents its vision of autonomous driving. Sealed off from the hustle and bustle of the fair, six spherical glass cocoons attract attention. Surrounded by a 360-degree screen, visitors get the impression of moving through a futuristic city. The cocoons adapt their equipment to the wishes of the passengers. Accompanied by the A.I. Maia, passengers find four sample modes that allow them to do sports, to educate themselves, to work or to shop by drone while driving. Travel time becomes valuable leisure time. For example, in the sports mode visitors take part in a rowing race. Extendable handles serve as rudders; projections on the windscreen show the progress of the race. The discovery mode offers one of the visual highlights: the visitors get to know the vastness of our galaxy through a cinematic presentation. They then test their newly acquired knowledge in a quiz. The visitors are actively involved and experience how to use travelling time alternatively.

ATELIER MARKGRAPH

Stefan Weil, Prof. Lars Uwe Bleher, Tom Schubert

STEP INSIDE THE STORY: Analog, digital, hybrid

Atelier Markgraph ist eine inhabergeführte Agentur für Marken- und Themenerlebnisse im analogen und digitalen Raum. Von der Ausstellung über den Showroom bis hin zum interaktiven Format oder der cross-medialen Markenkommunikation – im Zentrum steht das Erlebbarmachen von Inhalten. Analog, digital, hybrid – formatoffen seit der Gründung 1986. Das Atelier wandelt stets an Grenzen: zwischen dem Permanenten und dem Temporären, zwischen Analogem und Digitalem, zwischen Fundiertem und Experimentellem, zwischen Corporate und Culture. Der agile Kreationsprozess wird von Projekt zu Projekt neu ausgestaltet. So entstehen immer neue, passgenaue Ideen und Formate. Gemein ist allen Projekten, dass die Arbeit daran vier Prinzipien folgt: UNDERSTAND, TRANSFORM, CONNECT UND FASCINATE. Diese strukturieren den Prozess eines jeden Projektes von Markgraph. Anhand exemplarischer Beispiele wird im Folgenden auf die einzelnen Schritte eingegangen.

STEP INSIDE THE STORY: analogue, digital, hybrid

Atelier Markgraph is an owner-managed agency for brand and theme experiences in analogue and digital spaces. From the exhibition and showroom to the interactive format or cross-media brand communication - the focus lays on bringing content to life. Analogue, digital, hybrid - open formats since the foundation in 1986. The Atelier is constantly moving along the boundaries between the permanent and the temporary, between analogue and digital, between the profound and the experimental, between corporate and culture. The agile creation process is redesigned from project to project. This guarantees, new, perfectly fitting ideas and formats are always created. All projects have in common that they follow four principles: UNDERSTAND, TRANSFORM, CONNECT AND FASCINATE. Those structure the process of each project by Markgraph. The individual steps are described below on the basis of examples.

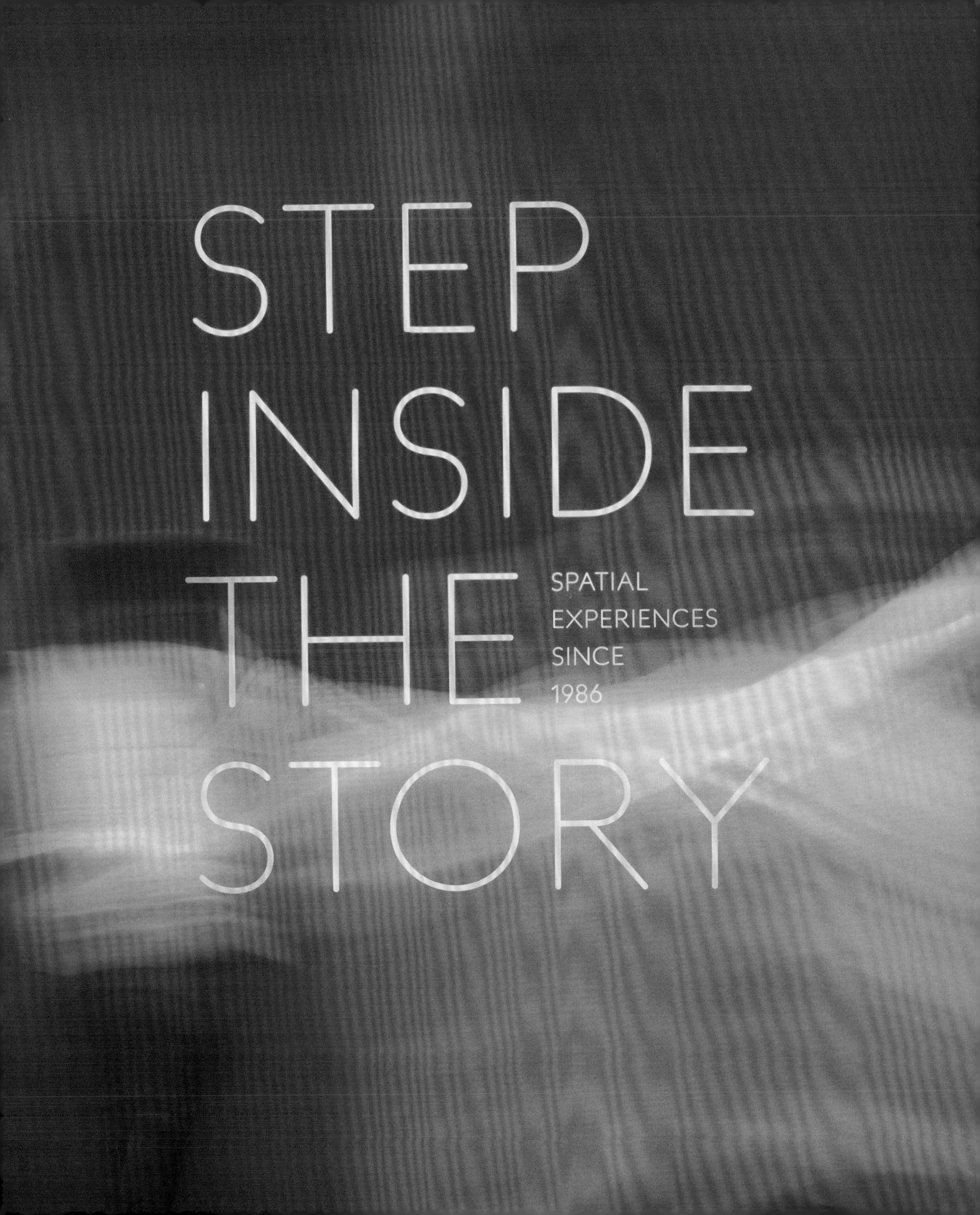

STEP INSIDE THE STORY

SPATIAL
EXPERIENCES
SINCE
1986

UNDERSTAND: KOMPLEXE INHALTE ERFASSEN UND VERSTÄNDLICH PRÄSENTIEREN

Am Anfang eines jeden Projektes steht die Durchdringung der Themen, Positionen und Beweggründe der Auftraggeber*innen. Je tiefer die fachspezifische Ergründung, umso wichtiger werden Antworten auf die Fragen nach dem kulturellen Kontext, nach der gesellschaftlichen Relevanz der Projektinhalte. Das Durchleuchten und Verknüpfen der Themen zu einem vielschichtigen Diskurs bildet die Basis für die gestalterische Arbeit. Die Jubiläumsausstellung „Selbst Denken" macht 200 Jahre nach der Veröffentlichung von Arthur Schopenhauers „Die Welt als Wille und Vorstellung" das Werk des Philosophen erlebbar. Er war davon überzeugt, dass der philosophische Diskurs in der Öffentlichkeit geführt werden muss, und seine Grundfragen sind bis heute ungeklärt. Deshalb beginnt die Ausstellung mit den aktuellen Widersprüchen und Fragen des Lebens. Diese leiten die Besucher*innen nahtlos in Schopenhauers Philosophie. Die Ausstellung wird zum begehbaren Gedankenraum, der Schopenhauers Strategie, Erkenntnis durch Perspektivwechsel zu gewinnen, erfahrbar macht. Multicodierte Installationen und Exponate bieten Schopenhauer-Neulingen und Expert*innen zahlreiche Anlässe und Anstöße zum Weiterdenken.

UNDERSTAND: CAPTURING COMPLEX CONTENT AND PRESENTING IT IN AN UNDERSTANDABLE WAY

Beginning each project, the client's themes, positions and motivations must be penetrated. The deeper the subject-specific investigation, the more essential it becomes to find answers to questions about the cultural context and the social significance of the project content. Investigating and linking the topics to form a multilayered discourse provides the basis for the creative work. The anniversary exhibition "Self Thinking" brings the philosopher's work to life 200 years after the publication of Arthur Schopenhauer's "The World as Will and Imagination". He was convinced that philosophical discourse had to be conducted in public, and his fundamental questions are still unanswered today. Therefore, the exhibition begins with the current challenges and questions of life. They guide visitors seamlessly into Schopenhauer's philosophy. The exhibition becomes a walk-in thought space that allows visitors to experience Schopenhauer's strategy of gaining insight through a change of perspective. Multicoded installations and exhibits offer Schopenhauer newcomers and experts alike numerous occasions and impulses to think further.

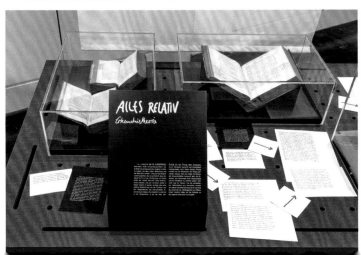

TRANSFORM: INTERDISZIPLINÄRE KREATION

Die zuvor erarbeiteten Inhalte werden in einem Konzept verdichtet und gestalterisch in den analogen oder digitalen Raum übertragen. Dies geschieht interdisziplinär in einem Team von Expert*innen unterschiedlicher Fachrichtungen: Architektur, Gestaltung, Redaktion, Strategie, Kommunikation, Technologie, Konzeption, Projektleitung, Software-Entwicklung, Filmproduktion, Wissenschaft und mehr. Ein großes Netzwerk aus Studios, Büros und Freelancern ergänzt die internen Kompetenzen. Für das FI-Forum, die Hausmesse der Finanz Informatik, entwickelt Atelier Markgraph eine zeitgemäße Architektur- und Gestaltungssprache. Die Schwarmintelligenz des Sparkassenverbunds wird in Form einer Soffittenstaffel in den Raum übersetzt und eine offene und dialogorientierte Workshop-Landschaft gestaltet. Und auch das Atelier profitiert in diesem Projekt von der Intelligenz der Vielen. Denn mithilfe eines engagierten Netzwerks wird ein facettenreiches Innovations- und Inspirationsprogramm für das FI-Forum kuratiert: von namhaften Gastredner*innen über Robotik- oder KI-Künstler*innen bis hin zu modernsten Technologie-Trends. Kooperieren statt Konkurrieren.

TRANSFORM: INTERDISCIPLINARY CREATION

The pre-developed content is condensed into a concept and transferred to the analogue or digital space in terms of design. This is done in an interdisciplinary way by a team of experts from different fields: architecture, design, editing, strategy, communication, technology, conception, project management, software development, film production, science and more. A large network of studios, offices and freelancers complements the internal fields. For the FI-Forum, the in-house exhibition of Finanz Informatik, Atelier Markgraph developed a contemporary architectural and design language. The swarm intelligence of the savings bank association is translated into the space in the form of a festoon relay and an open, dialogue-oriented workshop landscape is designed. The Atelier also benefits from the intelligence of the many in this project. With the help of a committed network, a multi-faceted innovation and inspiration programme is curated for the FI-Forum: from renowned guest speakers to robotics or AI artists to the latest technology trends. Cooperate instead of compete.

CONNECT: HYBRIDE ERLEBNISSE

In seinen Projekten verbindet das Atelier Markgraph seit jeher das Analoge mit dem Digitalen. Einerseits entstehen in analogen Inszenierungen einzigartige Momente des gemeinsamen Erlebens. Gleichzeitig helfen digitale Technologien dabei, Storytelling zu begleiten und zu verstärken und Menschen darüber hinaus nachhaltig miteinander in Kontakt zu bringen. Für den Austausch mit Fachexpert*innen und Partner*innen kreiert Atelier Markgraph für den Energiesystem-Hersteller Viessmann hybride Kommunikationsräume. Die begrünte „Partnership Lane" bietet vielfältige Gelegenheiten zum Austauschen und Netzwerken im direkten und zukunftsorientierten Miteinander. In den „Living Spaces", die die Lebensräume der Nutzer*innen darstellen, präsentieren Viessmann-Expert*innen Energie-Lösungen von der Brennstoffzelle im modernisierten Altbau bis zur Quartiers-Lösung, die ganze Wohnviertel mit Wärme versorgt. Mediale Trompe-l'oeils verbinden sich mit einem thematisch gestalteten Interior Design zu einem didaktischen, digital-analogen Kommunikationsraum. Darüber hinaus verdichtet eine Augmented-Reality-Show die Kernbotschaften des Markenauftritts. Mithilfe eines Stadtmodells sowie einer robotergesteuerten Kamera werden individuelle Lösungen und Prozesse sichtbar gemacht.

CONNECT: HYBRID EXPERIENCES

In its projects, Atelier Markgraph has always combined the analogue with the digital. On the one hand, analogue productions create unique moments of shared experience. At the same time, digital technologies help to accompany and intensify the storytelling process and also bring people into lasting contact with each other. Atelier Markgraph created hybrid communication spaces for the energy system manufacturer Viessmann for the exchange with experts and partners. The green "Partnership Lane" offers a variety of opportunities for exchange and networking in direct and future-oriented cooperation. In the "Living Spaces", which represent the homes of the users, Viessmann experts present energy solutions ranging from fuel cells in modernised buildings to neighbourhood solutions that supply entire residential areas with heat. Media trompe-l'oeils are combined with a thematically designed interior to create a didactic, digital-analogue communication space. In addition, an augmented reality show intensifies the core messages of the brand presentation. With the help of a city model and a robotic-controlled camera, individual solutions and processes are made visible.

Solutions for commerce and local authorities

development of new business areas for contractors

Dialogzone Dialogue zone

Frage der Stunde
Question of the hour

FASCINATE: NACHHALTIGE BEGEISTERUNG

Das Atelier schafft Momente, die nachhaltig berühren. Menschen sollen die Themen und Botschaften der Auftraggeber*innen nicht nur verstehen, sondern von ihnen begeistert werden. Das Faszinierende an einem Thema herauszukitzeln und in ein eindrucksvolles und nachklingendes Erlebnis zu übersetzen, ist das höchste Ziel. Dabei verschiebt Markgraph immer wieder Grenzen und entwickelt immer neue Perspektiven und Formate. Besucher*innen der Mercedes-Benz Experience betreten keine traditionelle Fahrzeugausstellung, sondern immersive Zukukunftsszenarien – ein Paradigmenwechsel, der die Wünsche der Zielgruppe fokussiert. In vier Themenbereichen durchlaufen sie eine partizipative Experience, die die ökologischen, sozialen und technologischen Implikationen der Mobilität von morgen thematisiert und Lust macht, diese auszuprobieren. Die mediale Fassade der Themenbereiche wiederum kreiert ein fulminantes Gesamtbild, das „Big Picture". Dieses bildet die Kulisse für eine nahbare Inszenierung der Show-Fahrzeuge. Durch die Kombination von Film und Live-Auftritt entsteht eine neue Form der Echtzeit-Kommunikation. Das vielfach ausgezeichnete Projekt wurde in Co-Creation mit jangled nerves entwickelt.

FASCINATE: SUSTAINED ENTHUSIASM

The Atelier creates moments that have a lasting effect. People should not only understand the themes and messages of the clients, but also be inspired by them. The highest goal is to extract the fascination of a topic and translate it into an impressive and resonant experience. Thereby, Markgraph is constantly shifting boundaries and developing new perspectives and formats. Visitors of the Mercedes-Benz Experience do not enter a traditional vehicle exhibition, but immersive future scenarios - a paradigm shift that focuses on the needs of the target group. In four thematic areas, the visitors pass through a participatory experience that explores the ecological, social and technological implications of tomorrow's mobility and makes them want participate. The media facade of the thematic areas in turn creates a brilliant overall picture, the "Big Picture". This forms the backdrop for an approachable staging of the show vehicles. The combination of film and live performance creates a new form of real-time communication. The award-winning project was developed in co-creation with jangled nerves.

BRANDHERM + KRUMREY

Susanne Brandherm & Sabine Krumrey
with students from AMD Academy Fashion and Design in Hamburg

Mit Büros in Köln und Hamburg ist brandherm + krumrey eines der renommiertesten Büros für Innenarchitektur in Deutschland. Das 1999 von Susanne Brandherm und Sabine Krumrey gegründete Büro realisiert internationale Projekte, die mit zahlreichen Preisen ausgezeichnet wurden. Ein Team von 26 Innenarchitekten, Architekten und Grafikern Designer sind verantwortlich für die Umsetzung maßgeschneiderter Designideen. Die Hauptarbeitsbereiche umfassen große Projekte wie Büros, Hotels und Krankenhäuser für bekannte Kunden. Darüber hinaus entwirft das Büro auch Ausstellungsräume, Arztpraxen, und Apotheken oder spezielle Privathäuser. Susanne Brandherm und Sabine Krumrey arbeiten nicht nur mit Vorträgen und Jury-Aktivitäten, sondern auch an speziellen Aufgaben wie Präsentationskonzepten zu Themen wie Coworking oder neuen Arbeitsumgebungen. Sabine Krumrey ist seit März 2015 Dozentin in der Abteilung „Interior Concepts and Design" an der AMD Academy Fashion and Design in Hamburg.

With offices in Cologne and Hamburg, brandherm + krumrey is one of the most renowned offices for interior design in Germany. Founded in 1999 by Susanne Brandherm and Sabine Krumrey, the office realises international projects that have won numerous awards. A team of 26 interior designers, architects, and graphic designers is responsible for the implementation of tailor-made design ideas. The main areas of work include large projects such as offices, hotels, and hospitals for well-known clients. In addition, the office also designs showrooms, medical practices, and pharmacies or special private residences. In addition to busy lecturing and jury activities, Susanne Brandherm and Sabine Krumrey also work on special tasks such as presentation concepts on topics like coworking or new working environments. Sabine Krumrey has also been a lecturer in the „Interior Concepts and Design" department at AMD Academy Fashion and Design in Hamburg since March 2015.

WORK TO GO

DRIVEN BY

AITDIALOG

amd

brandherm + krumrey
interior architecture

HOSTED BY

koelnmesse   ORGATEC

POWERED BY

Steelcase
viccarbe
Bolia·com
coalesse
Interface
GIRA
ZUMTOBEL
PolyVision
PFLEIDERER
sodexo
Microsoft
création baumann

WORK TO GO – ZUKUNFTSWEISENDE THEMENWELT - ORGATEC 2018, KOELNMESSE

Anlässlich der internationalen Leitmesse Orgatec, widmeten sich brandherm + krumrey in Partnerschaft mit Kristina Bacht von AIT-Dialog, Studierenden der AMD Akademie Mode & Design Hamburg und Joachim Müller- Wedekind von der Steelcase AG sowie weiteren Partnern aus der Objektindustrie zukünftigen Arbeitswelten. Auf der Sonderfläche WORK TO GO, initiiert von der KölnMesse wurden Visionen für das Arbeiten von morgen gezeigt. Die vielfältig gestaltete Rauminstallation bot mit Vorträgen, Workshops und Diskussionen ein inspirierendes Forum. Die erstmals im Rahmen der Orgatec veranstaltete Sonderschau prä-sentierte die Vorstellungen einer jungen Generation für das Arbeiten der Zukunft. Auf der Sonderfläche WORK TO GO, initiiert von der Koelnmesse wurden Visionen für das Arbeiten von morgen gezeigt. Die vielfältig gestaltete Rauminstallation bot mit Vorträgen, Work-shops und Diskussionen ein inspirierendes Forum. Die erstmals im Rahmen der Orgatec veranstaltete Son-derschau präsentierte die Vorstellungen einer jungen Generation für das Arbeiten der Zukunft. Als Dozentin der AMD Akademie Mode & Design entwickelte Sabine Krumrey, brandherm + krumrey zusammen mit Studie-renden und den Partnern AIT-Dialog und der Steelcase AG das Standkonzept, das auf 400 Quadratmetern eine anregende Themenfläche inszenierte.

WORK TO GO - FORWARD-LOOKING THEME WORLD - ORGATEC 2018, KOELNMESSE

On the occasion of the leading international trade fair Orgatec, brandherm + krumrey, in partnership with Kristina Bacht from AIT-Dialog, students of the AMD Akademie Mode & Design Hamburg and Joachim Mül-ler-Wedekind from Steelcase AG and other partners from the contract industry, dedicated themselves to fu-ture working environments. In the special area WORK TO GO, initiated by KölnMesse, visions for the work of tomorrow were shown. The diverse room installation offered an inspiring forum with lectures, workshops and discussions. The special show, held for the first time as part of Orgatec, presented the ideas of a young generation for the work of the future. Visions for to-morrow's work were shown on the special WORK TO GO area, initiated by Koelnmesse. The diverse room installation offered an inspiring forum with lectures, workshops and discussions. The special show held for the first time as part of Orgatec presented the ideas of a young generation for the work of the future. As a lecturer at the AMD Akademie Mode & Design, Sabine Krumrey, brandherm + krumrey, together with students and partners AIT-Dialog and Steelcase AG, developed the stand concept, which staged an exciting themed area on 400 square meters.

CBA CLEMENS BACHMANN ARCHITEKTEN

Clemens Bachmann

Das Büro CBA Clemens Bachmann Architekten wurde 2004 von Clemens Bachmann in München gegründet. CBA bearbeitet Projekte unterschiedlichster Größe aus den Bereichen Hochbau-Architektur, Innenarchitektur und Design. In den vergangenen 15 Jahren konnte das Büro eine Vielzahl von Projekten national und international im Bereich Innenarchitektur Fußballstadien, Büroumbauten oder Großgastronomie realisieren. Zu den Aufträgen im Hochbau zählen Sanierungen und Umbauten von Wohngebäuden, Umnutzungen im Denkmalschutz sowie Ein- und Mehrfamilienhäuser. Das internationale Team setzt sich aus Architekten, Innenarchitekten, Werksstudenten und Praktikanten sowie einem Netzwerk aus Fachplanern zusammen.

The office CBA Clemens Bachmann Architekten was founded in Munich in 2004 by Clemens Bachmann. CBA works on projects in the fields of building construction architecture, interior architecture and design. In the past 15 years the office has been able to make a large number of projects nationally and internationally in the fields of interior design, office conversions and restaurants. Among the orders in the building construction sector are the renovation and conversion of residential buildings, conversions in historic preservation as well as single and multi-family houses. The international team is made up of architects, interior designers, working students and interns as well as a network of specialist planners.

EINE AUSSTELLUNG IN KOOPERATION MIT DEM GASTEIG MÜNCHEN

Durch umgekehrt v-förmig aufgestellte Seekieferplatten wird der Raum zoniert und in Funktionsbereiche aufgeteilt. Die aus dem Raster herausgedrehten Ausstellungswände dienen zur Präsentation der Projekte. Ein Auditorium mit großer Projektionsfläche gegenüber des Eingangs wird für Vorträge genutzt. Dieser Bereich hebt sich zusätzlich durch eine Teppichinsel von der restlichen Ausstellungsfläche ab. Auf großen Holztischen in der Mitte des Raumes und neben dem Eingang werden die Architekturmodelle zu den jeweiligen Projekten ausgestellt. Die industrielle Decke mit einer Vielzahl von haustechnischen Einbauten bleibt sichtbar und unterstreicht damit die zurückhaltende, improvisiert wirkende Ausstellungsarchitektur. Die Bestandsbeleuchtung des Raumes, ein einfaches, abgehängtes Leuchtstoffröhrenraster dient zur Ausleuchtung des Raumes. Auffolierte Bodenstreifen markieren die drei Kernprojekte der Ausstellung und folgen mit ihrem 45 Grad Winkel dem Raster der Ausstellungswände.

AN EXHIBITION IN COOPERATION WITH THE GASTEIG MUNICH

The room is zoned and divided into functional areas by reversed v-shaped sea pine slabs. The exhibition walls, which are turned out of the grid, present the projects. An auditorium with projection screen opposite the entrance is used for lectures. This area also stands out from the rest of the exhibition space with a carpet island. On wooden tables in the middle of the room and next to the entrance the architectural models of the respective projects are exhibited. The industrial ceiling with its numerous technical installations remains visible, underlining the restrained exhibition architecture. The existing lighting, a simple, suspended fluorescent tube grid serves to illuminate the room. Foil-fitted strips of flooring mark the three core projects of the exhibition and, with their 45 degree angle, follow the grid of the exhibition walls.

Haus Holtmann

Standort: Köln, Deutschland
Jahr: 2007 – 2010
Auftraggeber: Dr. Klaus Holtmann
Größe: 350 m²
Status: fertiggestellt

18

COPYRIGHT COMMUNICATIONS

Christian Scholz & Ben Kunze

Ein offener Blick über den Tellerrand. Die Verknüpfung unterschiedlichster Perspektiven. Das Finden innovativer Lösungen und deren Umsetzung – dies sind nur einige der zentralen Punkte, die klarmachen, welche Philosophie Copyright Communications vertritt. Die Agentur für interdisziplinäres Design und Kommunikation im Raum betreut von Frankfurt am Main aus Markenauftritte, Events und Ausstellungen weltweit. Architekten, Programmierer und Motion-Designer, Redakteure, Exponat-Entwickler und Art-Direktoren arbeiten Hand in Hand unter einem Dach zusammen. Das garantiert kurze Wege und schnelle Entscheidungsfindungen. Und es sorgt ebenso für eine produktive Diskurskultur und eine intensive Arbeitsatmosphäre, in der Ideen geboren werden, die das Gewöhnliche weit hinter sich lassen. Als Mannschaft aus interdisziplinären Spezialisten steht Copyright Communications für den Gedanken, dass sich der Wert jedes einzelnen Teammitgliedes im Ergebnis der gemeinsamen Arbeit widerspiegelt.

An open view over the edge of the plate. The linking of the most diverse perspectives. Finding innovative solutions and implementing them are just a few of the central points that make it clear what Copyright Communications philosophy represents. From its base in Frankfurt am Main, the agency for interdisciplinary design and communication in space looks after brand presentations, events and exhibitions worldwide. Architects, programmers and motion designers, editors, exhibit developers and art directors work hand in hand under one roof. This guarantees short distances and fast decision-making. And it also ensures a productive culture of discourse and an intensive working atmosphere in which ideas are born that leave the ordinary far behind. As a team of interdisciplinary specialists, Copyright Communications stands for the idea that the value of each individual team member is reflected in the result of their joint work.

SLUSH CONFERENCE 2017

Man muss nicht immer auf maximalen Motorenlärm setzen, um sich Gehör zu verschaffen. Für die Slush 2017
gestaltete Copyright Communications den Markenauftritt der Porsche AG unter dem Motto „lead the conversation". Auf der Start-up und Tech Convention in Helsinki agierte der Sportwagenproduzent auf Augenhöhe
mit Besuchern und Fachpublikum und lud zum Dialog
über Design, Motorentwicklung und Digitalisierung.
Entsprechend wurde der Stand konzipiert und umgesetzt. Der Verzicht auf ein Standpodest diente dem
Abbau möglicher Hemmschwellen. Warme Materialien,
gerichtetes Licht und eine Sitzskulptur aus recycelten
Skateboards schufen eine einladende Atmosphäre und
förderten die Gesprächskultur. Da ein Porsche Auftritt
ohne Fahrzeug aber undenkbar bleibt, wurde „Carpool-
Content" implementiert. In einem Panamera Plug-in-
Hybrid wurden Besucher auf einem Scenic-Drive durch
die Stadt gefahren und konnten während der Fahrt
über zukunftsträchtige Themen diskutieren. Die Live-
Videos dieser Fahrten ließen sich direkt auf dem Stand
erleben, als Beweis, dass sich Nachhaltigkeit und Mobilität nicht ausschließen müssen.

SLUSH CONFERENCE 2017

You do not always have to rely on maximum engine
noise to make yourself heard. For the Slush 2017, Copyright Communications designed the brand identity of
Porsche AG under the motto "Lead the Conversation".
At the Start-up and Tech Convention in Helsinki, the
sports car manufacturer acted at eye level with visitors
and traders and invited them to a dialogue on design,
engine development and digitalization. The stand was
designed and implemented accordingly. The renun-
ciation of a stand platform served to reduce possible
inhibitions. Warm materials, directed light and a seating sculpture made of recycled skateboards created
an inviting atmosphere and promoted a culture of dis-
cussion. Since a Porsche appearance without a vehicle
remains unthinkable, a "Carpool-Content" was implemented. In a Panamera plug-in hybrid, visitors were
driven through the city on a scenic drive and were able
to discuss future-oriented topics while driving. The live
videos of these drives could be experienced directly at
the stand, as proof that sustainability and mobility do
not have to be opposite to each other.

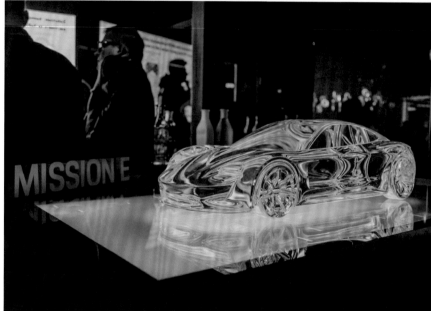

PORSCHE IAA 2017

Geschwindigkeit. Adrenalin. Herzrasen. Wenn man an Porsche denkt, dann denkt man an die Wildheit der Rennstrecke, an die Zuverlässigkeit und die überlegene Technik, die nötig ist, um das berauschende Gefühl einer Rekord-Runde in die Serie und den Alltag der Porsche Enthusiasten zu transponieren. Dieser Wille zur Performance ist tief in der Porsche DNA verwurzelt. Er schreibt sich fort in der Zukunftsagenda von Digitalisierung und Elektromobilität. Um diese Themen einfach und kraftvoll zu vereinen, entwickelte Copyright Communications für den Markenauftritt der Porsche AG auf der Internationalen Automobilausstellung 2017 in Frankfurt den „Code of Performance". Als Kommunikationsprinzip zog er sich wie ein roter Faden durch alle Bereiche des Messestandes und verband Grafik, Medien und Exponate zu einem umfassenden visuellen Erlebnis. Die komplexe Standarchitektur fesselte den Besucher mit ihrer auf Dynamik und Klarheit gerichteten Struktur und ließ ihn – nicht zuletzt dank der innovativen Exponate – zu einem aktiven Teil des Porsche Universums werden.

PORSCHE IAA 2017

Speed. Adrenaline. Tachycardia. When you think of Porsche, you think of the wildness of the race track, the reliability and the superior technology needed to transpose the exhilarating feeling of a record lap into the series and the everyday life of Porsche enthusiasts. This will to perform is deeply rooted in the Porsche DNA. It is carried forward in the future agenda of digitalisation and electromobility. In order to unite these topics in a simple and powerful way, Copyright Communications developed the "Code of Performance" for the brand presence of Porsche AG at the International Motor Show 2017 in Frankfurt. As a communication principle, it ran like a red thread through all areas of the trade fair stand and combined graphics, media and exhibits to create a comprehensive visual experience. The complex stand architecture captivated the visitor with its dynamic and clear structure and made him or her, thanks to the innovative exhibits, an active part of the Porsche universe.

TRATON AUF DER NFZ IAA 2018

Premieren haben ihren eigenen Reiz. Und sie bieten ganz besondere Herausforderungen. Um die TRATON Group bei ihrem ersten Auftritt auf der Nutzfahrzeuge IAA in Hannover 2018 ins rechte Licht zu rücken, musste Copyright Communications eine ebenso besondere Form der Präsentation verwirklichen. Die sich unter dem TRATON-Dach versammelnden Konzernmarken MAN, SCANIA, VWCO und RIO wurden durch verspiegelte, ringförmige Decken-elemente symbolisiert, deren Strahlkraft weit über den eigentlichen Stand hinausreichte. Durch die ausbalancierte Abstimmung der einzelnen Standbereiche gelang es, eine hohe Aufenthaltsqualität für den Besucher herzustellen. Die warmen, natürlichen Materialien, aus denen die unterschiedlichen Sitznischen und Podeste gefertigt waren, fungierten als Basis einer Atmosphäre der Gastfreundschaft –allen voran die Café-Bar als kommunikatives Zentrum des Standes. Die sich den unterschiedlichen Anforderungen anpassende Lichtinstallation sorgte dafür, dass sich der Besucher – ob auf der Ausstellungsfläche, in der Lounge oder vor der Konzertbühne – stets willkommen und am richtigen Platz fühlte.

TRATON AT THE NFZ IAA 2018

Premieres have their own charm. And they offer very special challenges. In order to put the TRATON Group in the right light for its first appearance at the IAA Commercial Vehicles in Hanover 2018, Copyright Communications had to think an equally special form of presentation. The group brands MAN, SCANIA, VWCO and RIO, which were gathered under the TRATON roof, were symbolised by mirrored, ring-shaped ceiling elements whose radiant power extended far beyond the actual stand. Through the balanced coordination of the individual stand areas, it was possible to create a high quality of stay for the visitors. The warm, natural materials used for the various seating niches and platforms served as the basis for an atmosphere of hospitality with a café-bar as the communicative centre of the stand. The lighting installation, which could be adapted to suit the various requirements, ensured that the visitor, whether in the exhibition area, in the lounge or in front of the concert stage, always felt welcome and in the right place.

Faces of TRATON

WEB SUMMIT 2019

„To the quiet mind, all things are possible." In einer Umgebung, die auf maximale Erregung von Aufmerksamkeit getrimmt ist, in der alles „Lauter!", „Schneller!", „Bunter!" schreit und Auffallen um jeden Preis zum Standard gehört, schlug Porsche eine ganz andere Richtung ein. Beim Web Summit 2019 in Lissabon, eine der wichtigsten Tech und Start-up Conventions Europas, entwickelte Copyright Communications für den Sportwagenhersteller eine Platt-form, die dem Besucher ein unwiderstehliches Rückzugsangebot machte: Einkehr, Entspannung, Re-Fokussierung. Hierfür musste die entsprechende Standumgebung geschaffen werden. Dies gelang durch Reduktion auf das Wesentliche und unter Verzicht auf alles visuell Ablenkende. Eine (Meta)Architektur aus Licht und transluzenten Vorhängen, aus schallabsorbierenden Materialien und einem Soundhintergrund, der störende Umgebungsgeräusche ausblendete, garantierten dem Besucher ein beruhigendes Ambiente. Sein Smartphone abzugeben, die Noise-Cancelling Kopfhörer aufzusetzen und sich in die Obhut international bekannter Meditationsexperten zu begeben, stellte eine völlig neue Erfahrung dar.

WEB SUMMIT 2019

"To the quiet mind, all things are possible. In an environment designed for maximum attention, where everything screams "Louder!", "Faster!", "More colorful!" and attention is standard at all costs, Porsche took a completely dif-ferent direction. At the Web Summit 2019 in Lisbon, one of the most important tech and start-up conventions in Europe, Copyright Communications developed a platform for the sports car manufacturer that offered visitors an irresistible retreat: contemplation, relaxation, refocusing. For this, the appropriate stand environment had to be cre-ated. This was achieved by reducing to the essentials and dispensing with anything visually distracting. A (meta) architecture of light and translucent curtains, of sound-absorbing materials and a sound background that fades out disturbing ambient noises guaranteed a calming ambience for the visitor. Handing over their smartphones, putting on the noise-canceling headphones and placing themselves in the care of internationally renowned meditation experts was a completely new experience.

DAYDREAMERS DESIGN

Stanley Siu

Alles Große beginnt mit Träumern; wir setzen unsere Kraft, Leidenschaft und unseren Beruf ein, um unsere Träume zu verwirklichen. daydreamers design ist ein junges, international preisgekröntes Architekturbüro mit Sitz in Hongkong, das eine Vision hat, die sich durch die Artikulation kreativer und alternativer Lösungen für die komplexen sozialen Herausforderungen unserer Zeit auszeichnet. Architektur ist ein Medium zur Schaffung einer besseren Gemeinschaft durch die Berücksichtigung des Kontexts, den Wunsch nach Exzellenz, Aufmerksamkeit für Details, innovative Designlösungen, nachhaltige Absichten, disziplinübergreifende Zusammenarbeit, Ideenaustausch und den Glauben an unsere Verantwortung, uns am sozialen Dialog zu beteiligen und unser Wissen in die Nachbarschaft und die Gemeinschaft einzubringen.

daydreamers design hat kreative Ideen in Hongkong, Australien, China, Italien, Macao, Malaysia, Taiwan, den Vereinigten Arabischen Emiraten und den USA umgesetzt. Unsere Dienstleistungen zielten darauf ab, die Wünsche, Bedürfnisse und Überzeugungen der Kunden durch Architekturdesign, Innenarchitektur, Kuration, Ausstellungsgestaltung, Installation, Kunstwerke und Gemeindeentwicklung zu erfüllen.

Every great thing begins with dreamers; we utilise our strength, passion and profession to reach for our dreams. daydreamers design is a young international award-winning architectural firm based in Hong Kong possess a vision that is characterised by articulating creative and alternative solutions to the complex social challenges today. Architecture is a medium to establish a better community through consideration of context, desire for excellence, attention to details, innovative design solutions, sustainable intentions, cross-discipline collaborations, ideas sharing and a belief in our responsibility to engage in social dialogue and contribute our knowledge back to the neighbourhood and community.

daydreamers design has executed creative ideas in Hong Kong, Australia, China, Italy, Macau, Malaysia, Taiwan, UAE and USA. Our services aimed to fulfil clients' aspirations, needs and beliefs via architectural design, interior design, curation, exhibition articulation, installation creation, artworks and community development.

DURCHQUEREN DER VERBOTENEN STADT - ARCHITEKTUR & HANDWERKSKUNST

Durchqueren der Verbotenen Stadt - Architektur & Handwerkskunst zielte darauf ab, das Konzept und die Verererbung, Bedeutung und Ästhetik der traditionellen chinesischen Architektur und Handwerkskunst zu präsentieren und zu vermitteln. Die Zeit vergeht, überdauert, aber historische Spuren bleiben. Hongkong ist mehr als 1.900 Kilometer von der Verbotenen Stadt entfernt. Diese Ausstellung konzentriert sich auf die Architektur und Handwerkskunst der Verbotenen Stadt. Als Drehscheibe für erstklassiges Handwerk und Ästhetik spiegelt sein geniales Design die exquisite Handwerkskunst und Kreativität dieser Zeit wider. Die Ausstellung zeigt die Details der handwerklichen Techniken, die zur Pracht der Verbotenen Stadt beigetragen haben. Im Laufe der Geschichte bleibt die faszinierende Landschaft der Verbotenen Stadt erhalten, die auf die hervorragenden Naturschutz-fähigkeiten zurückzuführen ist. Durch die Präsentation moderner Arbeiten, die mit traditionellen Techniken hergestellt wurden, und die Ausarbeitung des Einsatzes verschiedener Materialien, Verfahren und Werkzeuge zeigt diese Ausstellung die Konservierungsfähigkeiten, die über Generationen weitergegeben wurden.

TRAVERSING THE FORBIDDEN CITY – ARCHITECTURE & CRAFTSMANSHIP

Traversing the Forbidden City – Architecture & Craftsmanship aimed to present and educate the concept and Chinese traditional architecture and craftsmanship inheritance, importance and aesthetic. Time slips away regrets, but historical traces remain. Hong Kong is over 1,900 kilometres away from the Forbidden City. This exhibition focuses on the architecture and craftsmanship of the Forbidden City. As the hub of top-notch crafts and aesthetic, its ingenious design reflects the exquisite craftsmanship and creativity of that time. The exhibition showcases the details of the craftsmanship techniques which contributed to the magnificence of the Forbidden City. In the course of history, the Forbidden City's fascinating scenery remains, which attributed to the excellent conservation skills. Through the display of modern work made with traditional techniques and elaborating on the use of different materials, processes and tools, this exhibition reveals the conservation skills that have been passing down through generations.

HANG⁴ ZYU⁶ SIK⁶ ZI⁶ IN SEARCH OF HONG KONG'S LIGHT & SHADE, HONG KONG WEEK 2018 @ TAIPEI

In Hongkong greifen Ost und West in vielerlei Hinsicht ineinander und machen die Stadt zu einem florierenden kulturellen und kreativen Zentrum. Die Stadt ist mehr als ein blühender Kosmopolit. Wir haben ein starkes Gefühl für Hab und Gut, das durch Geschichte, Kultur, Sprache und Lebensstil gepflegt wird. In der Ausstellung erkundeten wir Hongkong anhand von Werbeanzeigen, Animationen und Installationsdesigns unter den Themen „Hang⁴" (Transport), „Zyu⁶" (Leben), „Sik⁶" (Lebensmittel) und „Zi⁶" (Sprache). In diesen vier Dimensionen identifizierten sich die Aussteller, nutzten ihre Kreativität, um Hongkong auszudrücken und zu präsentieren. 14 junge Kreativgruppen erkundeten die Stadt erneut und schufen eine Reihe interaktiver Multimedia-Exponate, die im Huashan 1914 Creative Park in Taipeh, Taiwan, ausgestellt wurden. Aristoteles sagte einmal: „Der Mensch ist ein zielstrebiges Tier. Sein Leben hat nur dann einen Sinn, wenn er nach seinen Zielen strebt." Wir alle suchen ständig nach unserer Identität, erkunden Hongkong und drücken unsere Perspektiven durch Kreativität aus.

HANG⁴ ZYU⁶ SIK⁶ ZI⁶ IN SEARCH OF HONG KONG'S LIGHT & SHADE, HONG KONG WEEK 2018 @ TAIPEI

In Hong Kong, East and West mesh in many ways, making the city a thriving cultural and creative hub. The city is more than a flourishing cosmopolitan. We have a strong sense of belongings cultivated via history, culture, language and lifestyle. In the exhibition, we explored Hong Kong through the advertisements, animations and installation designs under the theme of "Hang⁴" (Transportation), "Zyu⁶" (Living), "Sik⁶" (Food) and "Zi⁶" (Language). In these four dimensions, the exhibitors identified themselves, utilised their creativity to express and showcased Hong Kong. 14 young creative groups re-explored the city and created a series of multimedia exhibits showcased in the Huashan 1914 Creative Park, Taipei, Taiwan. Aristotle once said "Man is a goal-seeking animal. His life only has meaning if he is reaching out and striving for his goals". We are all continuously searching for our identity, exploring Hong Kong and expressing our perspectives via creativity.

STRATEGIEN IN DER ARCHITEKTUR HONG KONG IN VENEDIG AUF DER 15. INTERNATIONALEN ARCHITEKTURAUSSTELLUNG LA BIENNALE DI VENEZIA, 2016

Die 15. Internationale Architekturausstellung mit dem Titel REPORTING FROM THE FRONT, kuratiert von Alejandro Aravena und organisiert von der Biennale di Venezia unter dem Vorsitz von Paolo Baratta. Die Ausstellung wurde 2016 in den Veranstaltungsorten Giardini und Arsenale der Öffentlichkeit zugänglich gemacht. Die ausstellenden Architekten und Künstler untersuchten die Herausforderungen, denen sie gegenüberstehen, und versuchten, Lösungen für die Komplexität der Realität zu finden. Die Ausstellung in Hongkong bezog sich auf den klassischen chinesischen Aufsatz Sechsunddreißig Strategien. Jeder der jungen Aussteller ist einzigartig und hat seine Merkmale in der architektonischen Gestaltung oder Kunstschöpfung mit dem neuen moralischen Wert und sie sind die neue treibende Kraft unserer Gesellschaft. Als Antwort auf unsere kuratorische Erklärung zur Definition unseres „Frontier" (Schlachtfelds) haben sich die Aussteller mit den sechsunddreißig Strategien befasst. Sie wählten eine Strategie aus, um zu demonstrieren, wie er oder sie auf ihrem Schlachtfeld an der Grenze zwischen Architektur oder Kunst Erfolg haben würde.

STRATAGEMS IN ARCHITECTURE HONG KONG IN VENICE AT THE 15TH INTERNATIONAL ARCHITECTURAL EXHIBITION LA BIENNALE DI VENEZIA, 2016

The 15th International Architecture Exhibition, titled REPORTING FROM THE FRONT, curated by Alejandro Aravena and organized by La Biennale di Venezia chaired by Paolo Baratta. The exhibition opened to the public in 2016 at the Giardini and the Arsenale venues. The Hong Kong Exhibition drawing reference from classical Chinese essay Thirty-Six Stratagems, the exhibiting architects and artists examined the challenges they face and attempt to provide solutions to the complexity of reality. Each of the young exhibitors is unique and have their characteristics on the architectural design or art creation with the new moral value, and they are the new driving force of our society. In response to our curatorial statement regarding the definition of our "Frontier" [Battleground], the exhibitors looked into the Thirty-Six Stratagems. They selected one stratagem to demonstrate how he or she would succeed in their battleground at the frontier of architecture or art.

THE SILHOUETTE – SHANGHAI CHINESE INTERNATIONAL IMPORT EXPO, 2019

Wandern in der nostalgischen Welt von Hongkong, dem ikonischen Muster, das im Fluss der Geschichte und Kultur schwebt. Die kulturellen Symbole Hongkongs wie Architektur, Mode und Produktdesign manifestierten sich im 19. Jahrhundert.

„The Silhouette" hat die Serie von Hongkong-Mustern festgehalten und in einem zeitgenössischen Pavillon auf der Shanghai Chinese International Import Expo neu interpretiert. Die architektonische Struktur des Pavillons wurde von der spektakulären Stadtansicht von Hongkong inspiriert und mit 6 ausgewählten Metallrahmengeometrien dekoriert. Die Geometrien lösten sich vom Metallrahmen an Fenstern und Eingangstoren eines Mietshauses, Tong Lau, der Darstellung der Mischkultur. Die architektonischen Merkmale von Tong Lau wurden auf dem Metallrahmen, den Mosaikfliesen und der Beschilderung erläutert. Der 220 m² große, 6 m hohe Ausstellungspavillon präsentierte die kulturellen Symbole und Elemente unseres täglichen Lebens. Bitten Sie uns auch um die subtile Schönheit, die uns umgibt.

THE SILHOUETTE – SHANGHAI CHINESE INTERNATIONAL IMPORT EXPO, 2019

Wandering in the nostalgic world of Hong Kong, the iconic pattern floating in the river of history and culture. The cultural symbols of Hong Kong, such as architecture, fashion and product design, manifested in the 19th century.

"The Silhouette" captured the series of Hong Kong pattern and reinterpreted into a contemporary pavilion in Shanghai Chinese International Import Expo. The architectural structure of the pavilion inspired by the spectacular city view of Hong Kong and decorated with 6 selected metal frame's geometries. The geometries sifted from the metal frame on windows and entrance gates of a tenement building, Tong Lau, the representation of mix culture. The architectural features on Tong Lau explicated on the metal frame, mosaic tiles and signage. The 220 sqm, 6 m in height exhibition pavilion presented the cultural symbols and elements in our daily life. Also, requesting our attention to the subtle beauty surrounding us.

DESIGNBÜRO FÖN,DESIGN_

Arkas Förstner

Das 2003 von Dipl. Ing. FH FB Innenarchitektur Arkas Förstner gegründete Designbüro fön,design_ mit Sitz in Schramberg (Schwarzwald) gestaltet und realisiert Innenräume für Museen, Messen, Ausstellungen, Shops, Gastronomie sowie private Wohnräume. Bei den von fön,design_ entwickelten Konzeptionen stehen Information und Faszination gleichberechtigt im Fokus. Die Botschaft der Kunden wird durch eine perfekt inszenierte Visualisierung auf den Punkt gebracht. „Wir überraschen die Besucher und Gäste und wecken dadurch das Interesse an den Produkten und Exponaten." Die Entwürfe begeistern durch Kreativität, Originalität und Ausdrucksstärke. Das unterstreichen auch internationale Auszeichnungen für herausragende Designqualität. Eine intelligente Innenarchitektur sowie die gezielte Auswahl der Materialien berücksichtigen individuelle Vorgaben zur Präsentation der jeweiligen Marke/Exponat und zur Inszenierung ihrer Besonderheiten. Der intensive Austausch mit den Kunden ist die Basis für ein zielführendes Konzept und die spezifische Umsetzung inklusive Produktions- und Bauleitung vor Ort.

fön,design_, founded in 2003 by Dipl. Ing. FH FB Innenarchitektur Arkas Förstner and based in Schramberg (Black Forest), designs interiors for museums, trade fairs, exhibitions, shops, restaurants as well as private living spaces. The concepts developed focus equally on information and fascination. The customer's message is brought to the point by a perfectly staged visualisation. "We surprise visitors and guests and thereby arouse interest in the products and exhibits." The designs inspire through creativity, originality and expressiveness. This is also underlined by international awards for outstanding design quality. An intelligent interior design and the targeted selection of materials take into account individual specifications for the presentation of the respective brand/exhibit and the staging of its special features. The intensive exchange with the customer is the basis for a target-oriented concept and the specific implementation including production and construction management on site.

KECK MESSESTAND EUROSHOP,
FRANKFURT
AUSGEZEICHNETES MESSE- UND
AUSSTELLUNGSDESIGN

Ausstellungsgestaltung ist die Schnittstelle von Raum und Kommunikation. Für den Experten der Marken-inszenierung Firma KECK GmbH hat fön,design_ den Messestand auf der EuroShop konzipiert. Die Schwer-punkte lagen auf der Präsentation des neuen Corporate Designs sowie der Darstellung des kompletten Service-portfolios. Beide Bereiche wurden gekonnt kombiniert und das Corporate Design dank des konsequenten schwarz/weiß Farbkonzeptes deutlich erlebbar. Eine zentral platzierte Arbeitsstation diente als Präsentati-onsmodul. Dargestellt wurden die einzelnen Service-leistungen des Unternehmens digital und analog von der ersten Designskizze bis zum 3D VR Modell.

Für das Konzept des Messestandes erhielt fön,design_ den „red dot award 2017" und den German Brand Award im Bereich Messedesign sowie eine Nominie-rung für den German Design Award 2019.

KECK EXHIBITION STAND FOR EUROSHOP,
FRANKFURT
EXCELLENT TRADE FAIR AND
EXHIBITION DESIGN

Exhibition design is the interface between space and communication. fön,design_ designed the exhibition stand at the EuroShop for the experts of the brand staging company KECK GmbH. The focus was on the presentation of the new corporate design and the com-plete service portfolio. Both areas were skilfully com-bined and the corporate design could be clearly ex-perienced thanks to the consistent black/white colour concept. A centrally located workstation served as a presentation unit. The individual services of the com-pany were presented digitally and analogously from the first design sketch to the 3D VR model.

fön,design_ received the "Red Dot award 2017" as well as the German Brand Award in the field of trade fair design and a nomination for the German Design Award 2019 for its trade fair stand concept.

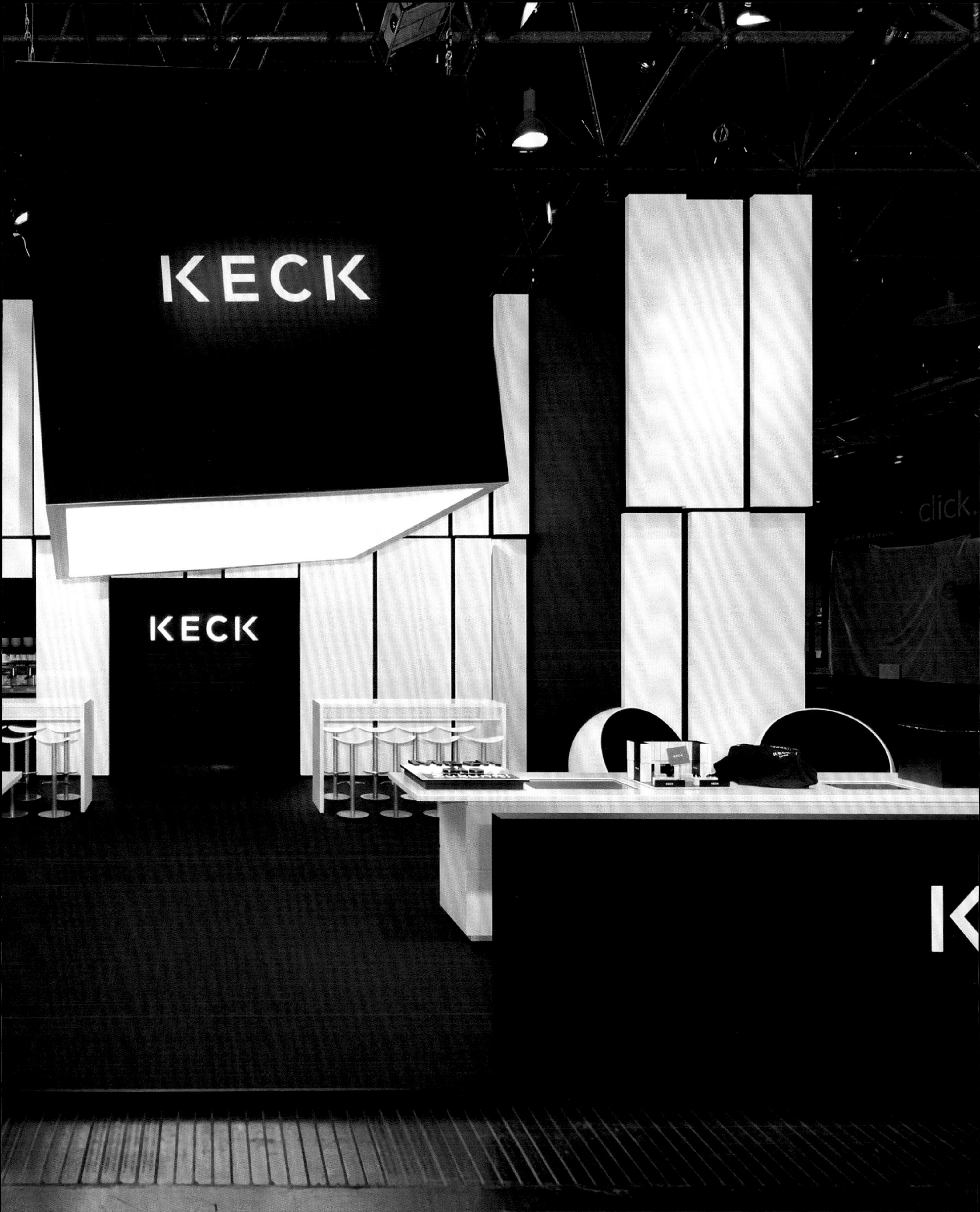
KECK
KECK
click.

HANSGROHE MESSESTAND ISH, FRANKFURT
DAS BESTE AUS ZWEI MARKENWELTEN

Ein Unternehmen – zwei Marken. Diese herausfordernde Aufgabenstellung für ein Messekonzept richtete der Bad-spezialist Hansgrohe an fön,design_. Ausgehend von einer „Zwei-Marken-Fassade" sollte im unverwechselbaren Ambiente der Frankfurter Festhalle die Führungsrolle der beiden Marken eindrucksvoll dargestellt werden. Die Lösung war eine medial bespielbare Fassade mit der Möglichkeit, die Präsentation der Marken in Intervallen zu wechseln. Eine besonders dominante Raumwirkung erzielte das Konzept durch die Aufteilung der 200 Quadrat-meter großen LED-Fläche in sieben einzelne Cluster, die im Raum gestaffelt abgehängt waren. Die farblich auf den jeweiligen Content abgestimmte Hinterleuchtung der Screens bot ein aufmerksamkeitsstarkes Umfeld der Dar-stellung. Im Innenbereich des fast 2000 Quadratmeter großen Messestandes waren die zwei Markenwelten dann streng getrennt. Eine individuelle Farb- und Materialauswahl verdeutlichte diese Differenzierung der Marken, die schließlich in der gemeinsamen Lounge wieder zu einer Einheit verschmolzen.

HANSGROHE EXHIBITION STAND FOR ISH, FRANKFURT
THE BEST OF TWO BRAND WORLDS

One company - two brands. This challenging task for a trade fair concept was assigned to fön,design_ by bathroom specialist Hansgrohe. Starting with an "two-brand-facade", the aim was to impressively demonstrate the leading role of the two brands in the unmistakable ambience of the Frankfurt Festhalle. The solution was a façade that could be used for media purposes with the possibility of changing the presentation of the brands at intervals. The concept achieved a particularly dominant spatial effect by dividing the 200 m² of LED surface into seven individual clusters, which were suspended in the room in a staggered manner. The backlighting of the screens, which was colour-coordinated with the respective content, provided an attention-grabbing environment for the presentation. The two brand worlds were then strictly separated in the interior of the almost 2.000 m² booth. An individual choice of colours and materials emphasised this differentiation of the brands, which merged into a single unit again in the shared lounge.

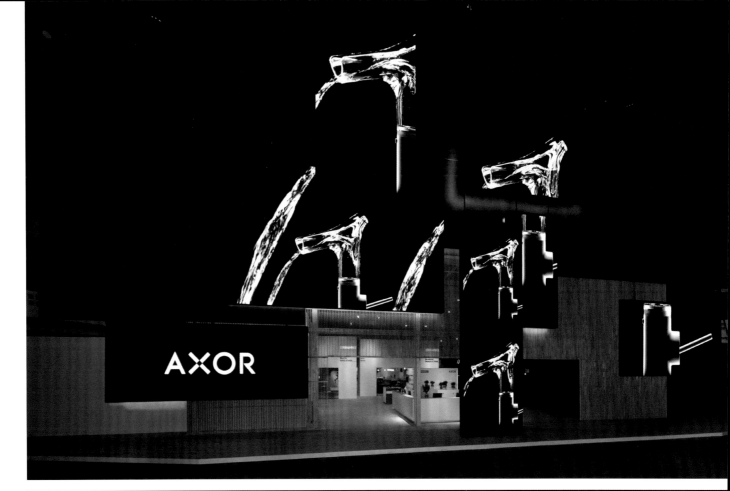

JUNGHANS TERRASSENBAU MUSEUM, SCHRAMBERG
MUSEEN ERZÄHLEN SPANNENDE GESCHICHTE(N)

Einzigartige Ausstellungsstücke, Interaktion sowie themenbezogene Führungen machen aus der Historie eine spannende Geschichte. Das Gesamtkunstwerk Museum erreicht seine Wirkung durch die stimmige Komposition aus Hülle, Inhalt und Präsentation. Beim Junghans Terrassenbau Museum ist zudem die außergewöhnliche Architektur des Gebäudes ein wichtiger konzeptioneller Teil der lebendigen Darstellung.

Große Teile des Museums in Schramberg (Schwarzwald) hat fön,design_ unter diesen Vorgaben konzipiert und realisiert. Dafür wurde ein übergreifendes Konzept entwickelt das informiert, fasziniert und überrascht. Das Leistungsspektrum geht über die reine Gestaltung und Baubetreung hinaus. So wurde auch das Exponathandling, Dokumentation, Grafik- und Texterstellung geleitet. Alle Stationen haben einen didaktischen und vermittelnden Hintergrund. Sie stehen für Dialog und Wissenstransfer und begeistern Besucher unterschiedlichen Alters durch differenzierte Ansprache. Verschiedene Medien schaffen die Verbindung zwischen Objekt und Betrachter. Das Junghans Terrassenbau Museum wurde für den Europäischen Museums Akademie Award und vom Europäischen Museums Forum für den EMYA Award nominiert.

JUNGHANS TERRASSENBAU MUSEUM, SCHRAMBERG
MUSEUMS TELL EXCITING STORIES

Unique exhibits, interaction, as well as theme-based guided tours turn history into an exciting story. The museum as a total work of art achieves its effect through the harmonious composition of shell, content and presentation. At the "Junghans Terrassenbau Museum", the building's architecture is also an important conceptual element.

Parts of the museum in Schramberg (Black Forest) were conceived by fön‚design_ under these specifications. A comprehensive concept was developed that informs, fascinates and surprises. The range of services goes beyond pure design and construction supervision. The handling of exhibits, documentation, graphic and text creation was also managed. Units stand for dialogue and transfer of knowledge and inspire visitors of different ages through differentiated approaches. Various media create the connection between object and viewer. The Junghans Terrassenbau Museum was nominated for the European Museums Academy Award and by the European Museums Forum for the EMYA Award.

FUHRIMANN HÄCHLER ARCHITEKTEN / LAUFEN BATHROOMS AG

Andreas Fuhrimann & Gabrielle Hächler

Andreas Fuhrimann und Gabrielle Hächler studierten Architektur an der ETH Zürich. Seit 1995 führen sie das Architekturstudio Fuhrimann Hächler in Zürich. Ihre Arbeiten zeichnen sich aus durch Interaktion mit der Umgebung, räumliche Komplexität, ökonomisch effektive Konstruktion, alltägliche, jedoch visuell anspruchsvolle Materialien und einen dezenten Hang zum Skulpturalen. Die Architektur des Studios ist konzeptuell durchdacht und wird dennoch immer wieder bewusst durch Nichtperfektion und mehrdeutige Materialien wie grob geschalten Beton, Kistensperrholz, aber auch spiegelnde, farbige Glasflächen durchbrochen. Es gehört zum Selbstverständnis der Architekten, Gegensätze zu kombinieren und mit den örtlichen kulturellen Gegebenheiten zu interagieren. Die beiden besitzen eine große Nähe zur Kunst, weswegen sich gerade Künstler, Kuratoren und kunstnahe Institutionen zu ihrer Architektur besonders hingezogen fühlen. Zu ihren bekanntesten und prämierten Bauwerken gehören das Haus Eva Presenhuber in Vnà und Haus Alder in Zürich, das Atelierhaus Müller Gritsch in Lenzburg, der Finish Tower Naturarena Rotsee in Luzern, das Künstlerhaus am Üetliberg und der Pavillon Hafen Riesbach in Zürich sowie das Friedhofsgebäude Erlenbach.

Andreas Fuhrimann and Gabrielle Hächler studied architecture at the ETH Zurich and since 1995 they have been running the Fuhrimann Hächler architectural studio in Zurich. Their work is characterised by its interaction with the environment, spatial complexity, economically effective construction utilising everyday but visually demanding materials and a discreet tendency towards the sculptural. The architecture of the studio is conceptually well thought-out, yet is repeatedly and deliberately broken up by imperfection and ambiguous materials such as coarsely layered concrete, box plywood, but also reflective, coloured glass. It is part of the architects' identity to combine opposites and seek inspiration from local cultural conditions. The pair have an affinity to art, which is why artists, curators and art-related institutions feel particularly drawn to their architecture. Among their most famous and award-winning buildings are the Haus Eva Presenhuber in Vnà and Haus Alder in Zurich, the Atelierhaus Müller Gritsch in Lenzburg, the Finish Tower Naturarena Rotsee in Lucerne, the Künstlerhaus on the Üetliberg and the Pavilion Hafen Riesbach in Zurich as well as the Erlenbach cemetery building.

LAUFEN MESSESTAND
SALONE DEL MOBILE 2018

Die Schweizer Architekten Andreas Fuhrimann und
Gabrielle Hächler haben sich mit dem Entwurf für den
Laufen Messestand auf dem Salone del Mobile Milano
2018 zum ersten Mal in ihrer Karriere an ein Ausstel-
lungsprojekt gewagt und einen ephemeren temporären
Raum gestaltet. „Für Laufen wollten wir ungewöhnli-
che, fast schon verfremdete, manchmal ironische, bizarre Elemente schaffen, die der Installation Leichtigkeit und eine kulturelle Dimension verleihen", erklären
die Architekten. Inspiriert vom Imagefilm sowie einem
Besuch in den Produktionsstätten, konzipierten die
beiden einen Stand, der sich um das Know-how des
Herstellers dreht und dessen reiche handwerkliche Tradition widerspiegelt. Der Stand zeigt einen deutlichen
Kontrast zwischen dem rauen Effekt der Wände und
den glänzenden Oberflächen der Ausstellungsstücke,
der durch eine lebhafte Farbpalette verstärkt wird. Im
Mittelpunkt der Installation steht eine Brunnen-Skulp-
tur, wie in einem arabischen Innenhof zelebriert sie das
Element Wasser. Wasser ist unentbehrlich bei der Her-
stellung von Keramik und geht bei der Nutzung eine Art
Symbiose mit den keramischen Objekten ein.

LAUFEN EXHIBITION STAND
SALONE DEL MOBILE 2018

With their inaugural design for the Laufen exhibition
stand at the Salone del Mobile Milano 2018, the Swiss
architects Andreas Fuhrimann and Gabrielle Hächler
have ventured into an exhibition project for the first
time in their career, creating an ephemeral temporary
space. "We wanted to create unusual, almost alien-
ated, sometimes ironic and bizarre elements, which
give the installation lightness and a cultural dimension",
explain the architects. Inspired by the award winning
Laufen image film and a visit to the production facili-
ties, the pair designed a stand that revolves around
the manufacturer's heritage and reflects its rich tradition of craftsmanship. The stand shows a clear contrast
between the rough effect of the walls and the glossy
surfaces of the exhibits, enhanced by a vibrant colour
palette. At the centre of the installation is a sculpture of
a fountain, as in an Arabic courtyard, it celebrates the
element of water. Water is indispensable in the production of ceramics, and when used enters into a kind of
symbiosis with the ceramic objects.

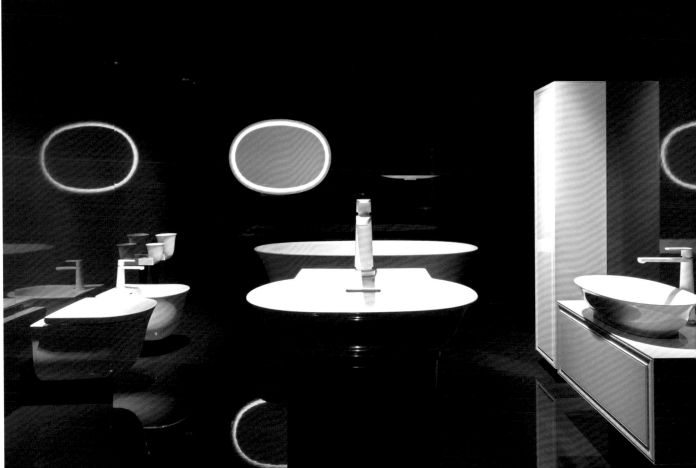

LAUFEN MESSESTAND ISH 2019

Unter der Federführung der Schweizer Architekten Andreas Fuhrimann und Gabrielle Hächler ist für die weltgrößte Sanitärmesse ISH 2019 in Frankfurt am Main ein Ausstellungskonzept entstanden, das die Wurzeln des Schweizer Badherstellers widerspiegelt und schon beim Betreten des Standes bewusst macht, dass Laufen zu den einfluss-reichsten Badausstattern weltweit gehört. Die Außenansicht ist dabei eng an den Produktionsprozess des Badher-stellers angelehnt: Während die Gebrauchsspuren am Haupteingang die Geschichte des Handwerks erahnen lassen, besitzen die gezeigten Negativformen die Qualität zeitgenössischer Skulpturen. Die industrielle Aufmachung mit zementgebundenen Spanplatten erinnert an Beton brut. Drei niedrige Eingänge führen in ein großes, zentrales Atrium, wo Videoprojektionen gezeigt werden. Augenzwinkern ruft der aus Dusch-WCs gestalte Brunnen hervor, in-spiriert vom Trevi Brunnen in Rom, welcher der warmen Atmosphäre des Atriums eine angenehme Frische verleiht. Der Brunnen ist auch ein Treppe, welche die Erschliessung des oberen Stockwerkes bewerkstelligt. Vom Atrium aus gelangt man in vier weitere Räume mit Hochglanz - Oberflächen, die den Produkten gewidmet sind. Sie stellen auf abstrakte Weise Badezimmer-Umgebungen dar und verleihen so den Produkten von Laufen eine künstlerische Dimension.

LAUFEN EXHIBITION STAND ISH 2019

Under the direction of the Swiss architects Andreas Fuhrimann and Gabrielle Hächler, an exhibition concept was de-veloped for the International Sanitary Trade Fair - ISH 2019 in Frankfurt reflecting the roots of the Swiss bathroom manufacturer and making visitors aware, as soon as they enter the stand, that Laufen is one of the most influential bathroom furnishers in the world. The vision was closely linked to the bathroom manufacturer's production process: while the materials at the main entrance give an idea of the history of the craft, the negative forms on display have the quality of contemporary sculptures. The industrial presentation with concrete-bonded particle board is remi-niscent of Beton. Three low entrances lead into a central atrium, where video projections are shown. The fountain, designed from shower toilets and inspired by the Trevi Fountain in Rome, gives a pleasant freshness to the warm atmosphere of the atrium. The fountain is also a staircase that provides access to the upper floor. From the atrium there are four more rooms with high gloss surfaces dedicated to the products. They represent bathroom environ-ments in an abstract way, giving an artistic dimension to Laufen products.

LAUFEN MESSESTAND
IMM COLOGNE 2020

Eine Zuspitzung des Messe-Konzepts findet sich auf der imm cologne 2020. Hier teilt sich die Ausstellungsfläche in zwei getrennte Bereiche: Auf der einen Seite präsentiert der Hersteller in Badezimmer ähnlichen, mit hochglänzenden, farbigen Oberflächen versehenen Räumen seine Kollektionen. Die Rückwand dieser Badsituationen bildet eine große Betonscheibe. Dahinter befindet sich das Gegenteil der Kleinteiligkeit: Eine große offene Freifläche tut sich auf, das Bad wird zur Bühne. Es entsteht eine surreale Wohnlandschaft, in der die Sanitärobjekte entsprechend ihrer skulpturalen Form neu arrangiert werden, Wanne wird Bett, WC wird Stuhl. Inspiriert ist diese Szenerie von dem italienisch-französischen Filmdrama Das Gespenst der Freiheit (Original: Le Fantôme de la liberté) des Regisseurs Luis Buñuel aus dem Jahr 1974. Hierin reiht sich eine skurrile Episode an die andere. Gemeinsam ist allen das Prinzip der verkehrten Welt.

LAUFEN EXHIBITION STAND
IMM COLOGNE 2020

The trade fair concept from Fuhrimann Hächler has culminated at the imm cologne 2020, where the exhibition area is divided into two separate zones: on the one hand, the manufacturer presented its collections in bathroom-like rooms with high gloss, coloured surfaces against a contrasting concrete backdrop whilst behind it is the opposite of the small rooms: a space opening up, where the bathroom becomes a stage. The result is a surreal living landscape in which the sanitary objects are rearranged according to their sculptural form, the bathtub becomes a bed, the toilet becomes a chair. This scene is inspired by the Italian-French film drama The Specter of Freedom (original: Le Fantôme de la liberté) by director Luis Buñuel from 1974, in which one bizarre episode follows another. What they all have in common is the principle of the unexpected upside-down world.

LAUFEN MESSESTAND SWISSBAU
BASEL 2020

Eine beeindruckende Ausstellungslandschaft schufen die Architekten Fuhrimann Hächler für den Gemeinschaftsstand der Unternehmen Laufen und Similor auf der Swissbau 2020 in Basel. Einmal mehr lebt der Messestand vom Kontrast unterschiedlicher Materialien, Oberflächenstrukturen, Farben und Lichtverhältnisse. Das gestalterische Narrativ ist die Gegenüberstellung von traditioneller Handwerkskunst und innovativen Technologien. Hierfür überspitzen Fuhrimann Hächler die bisher verwendeten Elemente, die bruchstückhaft immer wiederkehren, indem sie den Räumen neben offenen und geschlossenen Wänden eine weitere Komponente hinzufügen: Glasflächen erlauben Blicke in andere Räume, die aufgrund ihrer Farbigkeit die Exponate „dahinter" in einem surrealen Licht erscheinen lassen. Die gesamte Ausstellungsfläche ist gegliedert durch große Kuben, in denen die Produkte gezeigt werden und die darüber hinaus der ganzen Fläche in ihrer dominanten Länge und Größe eine klare Struktur mit eindeutigen Achsen geben. So werden die Exponate gegliedert und die Besucher können durch die räumliche Inszenierung flanieren wie durch eine Stadt.

LAUFEN EXHIBITION STAND SWISSBAU
BASEL 2020

The architects Fuhrimann Hächler created an impressive exhibition landscape for the combined stand of the companies Laufen and Similor at Swissbau 2020 in Basel. Once again, the exhibition stand thrives on the contrast between different materials, surface structures, colours and lighting conditions. The design narrative is the juxtaposition of traditional craftsmanship and innovative technologies. To this end, Fuhrimann Hächler exaggerates the previously used elements, which recur in fragments, by adding a further component to the rooms: Glass surfaces allow glimpses into other rooms, which due to their colourfulness allow the exhibits to appear in a surreal light. The entire exhibition area is divided by large cubes, in which the products are displayed, which also give the entire area a clear structure with unambiguous axes in its dominant length. In this way the exhibits are structured and visitors can stroll through the spatial staging as if they were in a city.

GIGLER HOLZ-DESIGN

Josef Gigler

Innovation trifft Raum

Zeitlich begrenzte Eventbauten, bleibende Ausstellungen und Einrichtungen, individuelle Möbel, Küchen, skulpturale Objekte oder Serienfertigungen – die Schreinerei GIGLER holz-design kombiniert die Leidenschaft für qualifiziertes Handwerk mit den neusten technischen Möglichkeiten. Von der Projektplanung bis zum kleinsten Detail vereint sich hier profundes Wissen zu einer Symbiose aus Tradition, Technik und Innovation. Ein Zusammenspiel, das ein selbstsicheres, mutiges Fortschreiten in Richtung zukünftiger Entwicklungen ermöglicht. Ein Denken über Konventionen hinaus, das vordefinierte Grenzen überschreiten lässt. Neues zu erschaffen. Zukunft zu gestalten durch eine interdisziplinäre Zusammenarbeit von Natur, dem Menschen und analoger sowie digitaler Technik. Im stetigen Wandel mit den Anforderungen der Zeit mitzugehen und neue Lösungen auf zeitgemäße Problematiken zu finden. Visionen Raum und Form zu geben. Denn alles ist möglich, wenn wir frei denken. Die Transkription der Natur. Frei in Form und Ausführung.

Innovation meets space

Temporary event buildings, permanent exhibitions and furnishings, individual furniture, kitchens, sculptural objects or series production - the carpentry GIGLER holz-design combines the passion for qualified craftsmanship with the latest technical possibilities. From project planning to the smallest detail, profound knowledge is combined here to a symbiosis of tradition, technology and innovation. An interplay that enables a self-confident, courageous progress towards future developments. A way of thinking beyond conventions that allows predefined limits to be crossed. To create something new. To shape the future through interdisciplinary cooperation between nature, mankind and analogue and digital technology. To keep up with the demands of the times and find new solutions. To give space and form to visions. Because everything is possible when we think freely. The transcription of nature. Free in form and execution.

AMBIENTE SHOPAUSBAU

Exklusive Designermöbel erfordern eine exklusive Präsentation. GIGLER holz-design realisierte die Innenaus-
stattung der neuen Geschäftsfiliale des renommierten
Möbelhauses AmbienteDirect. Diese vertreibt Marken-
Wohndesign und Designklassiker für ein stilvolles Zuhause auf internationaler Ebene. Ein Großprojekt der
Spitzenklasse mitten in Münchens Altstadt. Zu fertigen
war das Surrounding für die Präsentation und Ausstellung exquisiter Designmarken: Schaufensterpodeste,
die durch einen zurückgesetzten Sockel visuell schwe-
bend die Ausstellungsstücke zur Schau stellen. Ergo-
nomisch, funktionell gestaltete Theken aus fugenlosen
Mineralwerkstoffplatten, die mit ihrer indirekter, warm-
weißer LED-Beleuchtung Kunden empfangen. Pick-Up
Regale, Light-Boxes und Podeste, die als amorphe,
frei gestaltbare Quader in verschiedenen Größen und
Tiefen zur Präsentation dienen. Ein Treppenaufgang,
der mit seinem fugenlosem Monitoreinbau für visuelle Effekte sorgt. Trennwände in L-Form mit deren Hilfe
separate Universen für die unterschiedlichen Markenwelten kreiert werden können. Zusammengefasst: Ein
Innenausbau, der den Charakter und Charme der Produkte bestmöglich untermalt. Das Ergebnis: Schlicht,
mondän, hochwertig.

AMBIENTE SHOP EXTENSION

Exclusive designer furniture requires an exclusive presentation. GIGLER holz-design realized the interior design of the new branch of the renowned furniture store
AmbienteDirect. This company distributes branded living design and design classics for a stylish home on an
international level. A top class in the middle of Munich's
old town. Surrounding was to be produced for the presentation and exhibition of exquisite design brands: display window pedestals, which visually float the exhibits
through a recessed base. Ergonomically, functionally
designed counters made of seamless solid surface panels, which welcome customers with their indirect LED
lighting. Pick-up shelves, light boxes and pedestals,
which serve as amorphous, freely designable cuboids
in various depths for presentation. A staircase, which
provides visual effects with its seamless monitor installation. L-shaped partition walls that can be used to create separate universes for the different brand worlds.
Summarizing: an interior design that underlines the
character and charm of the products in the best possible way. The result: simple, sophisticated, high-quality.

FRIEDBERG MUSEUMSAUSBAU

GIGLER holz-design verwirklichte das vom Münchner Designbüro „Atelier hammerl & dannenberg" inszenierte Museumsinventar für das Wittelsbacher Schloss in Friedberg. Klar definierte, moderne Linien im Kontrast zu homogenen, mittelalterlichen Gewölben. Das Zusammenspiel aus entspiegeltem Sicherheitsglas, matt lackierten Holzwerkstoffplatten und indirekt beleuchteten Ausstellungskorpen bietet eine extravagante Präsentationsfläche für die historisch wertvollen Kostbarkeiten. Das Ausstellungsinventar präsentiert mitunter wertvolle Uhren aus dem 17. Jhdt, seltenes Fayance-Geschirr sowie sakrale Kunst und archeologische Fundstücke von der Steinzeit bis zum frühen Mittelalter. Ein einzigartiges Treffen von Moderne und Historie – heute und hier in einer mittelalterlichen Burganlage des 13 Jhdts.

FRIEDBERG MUSEUM EXPANSION

GIGLER holz-design realized the museum inventory for the Wittelsbach Castle in Friedberg, Germany, which was designed by the Munich design office "Atelier Hammerl & Dannenberg". Clearly defined, modern lines in contrast to homogeneous, medieval vaults. The interplay of anti-reflective safety glass, matt lacquered derived timber product boards and indirectly illuminated exhibition corps offers an extravagant presentation area for the historically valuable treasures. The exhibition inventory sometimes presents valuable clocks from the 17th century, rare faience tableware as well as sacred art and archeological finds from the Stone Age to the early Middle Ages. A unique meeting of modernity and history in a medieval castle of the 13th century.

LOKSCHUPPEN MUSEUMSAUSBAU

Die Saurierausstellung im Lokschuppen in Rosenheim lädt auf 1500 m² ein die Welt vergangener Ozeane zu erforschen. GIGLER holz-design realisiert den raumbildenden Ausbau sowie Vitrinen nach den Vorstellungen des Architekturbüros „Atelier Hammerl & Dannenberg". Eine planerisch sowie konstruktionstechnisch „gigantische" Projektrealisierung. Scheinbar Unmögliches wird hier zu Möglichem. Denn gebogene Formen, schräge Winkel sowie große Volumina sind genau das, was GIGLER neugierig macht. Mit Hilfe einer universellen Konstruktionssoftware konstruierten und koordinierten die Projektleiter der Schreinerei gleichzeitig an drei Rechnern den gesamten Produktionsablauf Hand in Hand. Ein besonderes Konstruktionshighlight: Die 4,5 m hohe, schwebende Erdzeitspirale, die den Besucher visuell und gefühlt in den Kreislauf der Erdzeitgeschichte ein- und entführt. Auf den Spuren der Geheimnisse der „Giganten der Meere" werden in und auf den Museumsausbauten über 200 Original-Fossilien präsentiert. Ein Projekt, das durch seine Komplexität in der Umsetzung die Qualitäten der Schreinerei GIGLER holz-design sichtbar werden lässt.

LOCOMOTIVE SHED MUSEUM EXTENSION

The dinosaur exhibition in the engine shed in Rosenheim invites you to explore the world of past oceans on 1.500 m². GIGLER holz-design made the interior design as well as the showcases according to the ideas of the architectural office "Atelier Hammerl & Dannenberg". The seemingly impossible becomes possible here. Curved forms, oblique angles and volumes are exactly what makes GIGLER special. With the help of universal design software, the project managers of the carpentry workshop simultaneously designed and coordinated the entire production process hand in hand on three computers. A special construction highlight: the 4.5 m high, floating earth time spiral, which visually and emotionally introduces and takes the visitor into the cycle of the earth time history. On the tracks of the secrets of the "Giganten of Meere" more than 200 original fossils are presented in and on the museum extensions. A project that, through its complexity in its implementation, makes the qualities of the carpentry GIGLER holz-design visible.

KUKA MESSEAUSBAU

Für den Messestand des Industrieroboterherstellers KUKA realisierte GIGLER holz-design die gigantischen Wände und Balken für die HMI, die weltweit wichtigste Industriemesse in Hannover. Die Dynamik der Robotik sollte durch futuristisches Design zum Ausdruck gebracht werden. Diese Idee wurde in gebogene und in sich verdrehte Wandelemente und Balken übertragen, deren Umsetzung die Innovativität der Produkte selbst widerspiegelt. Der Messeauftritt sollte genau das transportieren, wofür Roboter stehen: Präzision, Innovation, Perfektion. Wieder einmal stellte sich GIGLER holz-design der Herausforderung, das nahezu Unmögliche umzusetzen. Wie das Team schon so einige Male unter Beweis stellen durfte, kann es gerne etwas kompliziert werden. Genau das ist ihre Spezialität! Immer wieder fordern komplexe Aufgaben das Team heraus, neue Lösungen zu generieren. Basis für dieses Engagement ist modernstes Equipment sowie langjährige Erfahrung im Schreinerhandwerk.

KUKA TRADE FAIR EXTENSION

For the trade fair stand of the industrial robot manufacturer KUKA, GIGLER Holz-Design made the gigantic walls and beams for the HMI, the world's most important industrial trade fair in Hanover. The dynamic of robotics was to be expressed through futuristic design. This idea was translated into curved and twisted wall elements and beams, whose implementation reflects the innovativeness of the products themselves. The trade fair presentation was to convey exactly what robots stand for: precision, innovation, perfection. Once again, GIGLER Holz-Design took on the challenge of making the almost impossible. As the team has already proven a few times, things can get a bit complicated. And that is exactly their speciality! Again and again, complex tasks challenge the team to generate new solutions. The basis for this commitment is state-of-the-art equipment as well as many years of experience in carpentry.

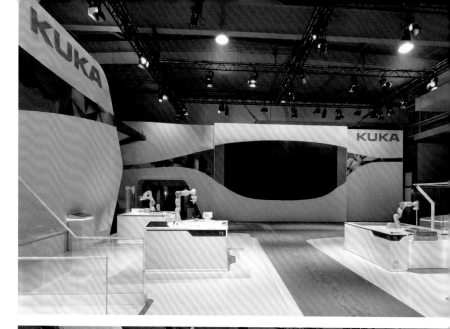

JOCHEN HUNGER MUSEUM & EXHIBITION DESIGN

Jochen Hunger

„Wir sind Agentur, Netzwerk, Werkstatt gleichzeitig. Im Kern überschaubar, mit viel erworbener Erfahrung, auch international. Wir entwickeln und bauen Ausstellungen, Exponate, beraten Museen, engagieren uns auch vor der Haustür für Know How Transfer und ein besseres Stadtklima."

„Die Werkstatt mit Lasercutter und anderen Prototyping Werkzeugen ist da, um Neues selbst zu entwickeln. Dorthin laden wir Gäste ein und experimentieren mit ihnen."

„Die besondere Befriedigung, die mit dem Selbermachen verbunden ist, das ist eine Energie, die uns interessiert."

„Ich glaube, dass es über das Selbermachen und das Vermitteln von Know-How möglich ist, auch die bekannt museumsfernen Gruppen, beispielsweise Teens, zu interessieren. Die Menschen heute wollen etwas mit sich selbst anstellen. Etwas Sinnvolles. Auch in der Ausstellung."

„Klarheit von Inhalt und Raum, Budget und Zeit. Besucher und Besucherin im Blick. Dieses Gerüst erlaubt dann, Fantasie, Kreativität und Wunder einziehen zu lassen."

We are agency, network and workshop at the same time; with much acquired experience, also internationally, we develop and build exhibitions, exhibits, advise museums, and are also committed to know-how transfer and a better urban climate on the doorstep.

Our workshop with lasercutter and other prototyping tools is there to develop new things by ourselves. We invite guests there and experiment with them.

"The special satisfaction associated with do-it-yourself is an energy that interests us."

"We believe that through do-it-yourself and the transfer of know-how, it is possible to interest groups who are not familiar with museums, such as teenagers. People today want to do something meaningful. Even when visiting an exhibition."

"Clarity of content and space, budget and time. Visitor in view. This framework allows imagination, creativity and wonder to move in."

BIBLIORAMA, DAS BIBELMUSEUM STUTTGART | 2015

Die Herausforderung: Wie lässt sich „das Buch der Bücher", die Bibel, in eine lebendige Dauerausstellung übertragen? Da die Besucher in diesem neu geschaffenen Museum eine aktive Rolle einnehmen sollten, schufen wir fünfzehn Orte, separate Bühnen, auf denen Protagonisten aus der Bibel und Besucher in einen Dialog kommen. Diese Bühnen haben bewusst unterschiedliche Merkmale, was Material, Farbe, eingesetzte Medien und Typographie betrifft. Einige liegen als Gärten im Freien, für den „Eva-Garten" wurde das Pflaster der Stadt aufgebrochen.

BIBLIORAMA, THE BIBLE MUSEUM STUTTGART | 2015

The challenge: How can "the book of books", the Bible, be turned into a living permanent exhibition? Since visitors should play an active role in this newly established museum, we created fifteen sites, separate stages, on which protagonists from the Bible and visitors enter into dialogue. These stages deliberately have different characteristics in terms of material, colour, media used and typography. Some of them are outdoor gardens; for the "Eva Garden" the city's pavement was broken up.

STADT – JUGEND – STIL | STADTMUSEUM WIESBADEN | 2019

Die Zeit um 1900 war voller technologischer, gesellschaftlicher und ästhetisch-künstlerischer Umbrüche. Für die Ausstellung nutzen wir ausgewählte Ausstellungsobjekte und farbige, leuchtende Wände mit plakativen Aussagen, um die Vielfalt und die Kraft dieser Umwälzung spürbar zu machen. Zwei Wahrnehmungsebenen: Erstmal wirken die intensive Farbigkeit und die Suggestion der zeitgenössischen Fotos, bei der Betrachtung aus der Nähe eröffnet sich die Vielfalt der lokalen Bezüge. Stereofoto-Betrachter zum räumlichen Blick in eine andere Zeit und eine App, mit der Besucher eigene Jugendstil-Muster erzeugen können, öffnen auch Schulkindern Zugänge in die jüngere Geschichte.

Die Herausforderung: Wie gelingt es, in einem sehr wuchtigen Raum sehr frische Aussagen zu machen?

CITY - YOUTH - STYLE | CITY MUSEUM WIESBADEN | 2019

The period around 1900 was full of technological, social and aesthetic-artistic transformations. For the exhibition we use selected exhibits and colored, luminous walls with striking statements to make the diversity and power of this upheaval tangible. Two levels of perception: First of all, the intense color and suggestion of contemporary photos make an impact; when viewed up close, the variety of local references opens up. Stereo photo viewers for a spatial view of another time and an app that allows visitors to create their own Art Nouveau patterns also open school children access to recent history.

The challenge: How to make very fresh statements in a very bulky room?

KREATIVSTUDIOS | EXPERIMENTA HEILBRONN | 2019

Im Herzen der neuen experimenta, Deutschlands nunmehr größtem Science Center, liegen die vier Kreativstudios. Sie sind thematisch inspiriert von den Ausstellungsgalerien, die sie umgeben, und unterscheiden sich in Ausstattung und Charakter. Ihre Ausstattung mit analogen und digitalen Werkzeugen macht sie zu unverwechselbaren Orten für Entdeckergeist und Kreativität. Die Herausforderung: Wie sehen Aktivitäten aus, die für Besucher aller Altersstufen ohne großes Vorwissen geeignet sind? Welche attraktiven Produkte zum Mitnehmen können entstehen?

CREATIVE STUDIOS | EXPERIMENTA HEILBRONN | 2019

The four creative studios are located in the heart of the new experimenta, now Germany's largest science centre. They are thematically inspired by the exhibition galleries that surround them, and are distinguished by their furnishings and character. Their equipment with analogue and digital tools makes them unmistakable places for the spirit of discovery and creativity. The challenge: What do activities look like that are suitable for visitors of all ages with little prior knowledge? And which attractive take-away products can be created?

JÜRGENSARCHITEKTEN

Natalie Jürgens

JÜRGENSARCHITEKTEN wurde 2007 von Natalie Jürgens gegründet. Unter dem Motto „Architektur für Unternehmen" betreut JÜRGENSARCHITEKTEN Unternehmen ganzheitlich in Sachen Messedesign, Events, neue Arbeitswelten, Showrooms – kurz: in allem, worin ein Unternehmen räumlich in Erscheinung tritt. Intensive Auseinandersetzung mit der Welt des Kunden und klare Kommunikation auf Augenhöhe vereinfacht den Arbeitsprozess und garantiert einen erfolgreichen Messeauftritt. Ganzheitlich heißt für JÜRGENSARCHITEKTEN auch, dass der Kunde bereits bei der Zielfindung, aber auch im Nachgang bei der Auswertung des Projekts unterstützt wird. 2019 hat JÜRGENSARCHITEKTEN beispielsweise eine umfassende Studie zum Thema „Effektivität von Messen" erarbeitet, bei der unter anderem klar wurde, dass nicht nur die Zielsetzung, sondern auch die Ergebniskontrolle nach der Messe ein heißes Thema in den Unternehmen ist. Aktuell hat JÜRGENSARCHITEKTEN die Studie 2020 um das momentan allgegenwärtige Thema „Messen und Corona" erweitert und ist in den intensiven Austausch mit Betroffenen getreten, um gemeinsam Lösungen und Alternativen zu erarbeiten. Am Ende sind es jedoch bei aller Professionalität einfach die Begeisterung und die Liebe zum schönsten Beruf der Welt, die JÜRGENSARCHITEKTEN tragen und die übrigens auch ansteckend sind...

JÜRGENSARCHITEKTEN was founded in 2007 by Natalie Jürgens. Under the motto "Architecture for Companies", JÜRGENSARCHITEKTEN supports companies holistically in terms of trade fair design, events, new working environments, showrooms - in short: in everything in which a company appears spatially. Intensive examination of the customer's world and clear communication at eye level simplify the work process and guarantee a successful trade fair appearance. For JÜRGENSARCHITEKTEN, holistic also means that the customer is supported not only in setting goals, but also afterwards in evaluating the project. In 2019, for example, JÜRGENSARCHITEKTEN developed a comprehensive study on the subject of "Effectiveness of trade fairs", which made it clear, among other things, that not only setting goals, but also monitoring results after the trade fair is a hot topic in companies. JÜRGENSARCHITEKTEN has recently expanded the 2020 study to include the currently ubiquitous topic of "trade fairs and corona" and has entered into an intensive exchange with those affected in order to work out solutions and alternatives together. In the end, however, despite all the professionalism, it is simply the enthusiasm and love for the most beautiful job in the world that JÜRGENSARCHITEKTEN carries and which, by the way, are also contagious ...

EUROSHOP 2020 FÜR PFLEIDERER

Eine kontinuierliche Zusammenarbeit bietet die Chance, das Messedesign immer weiter zu entwickeln – mal schrittweise aufeinander aufbauend, mal in größeren Sprüngen oder sogar Brüchen – je nachdem, wie der Werdegang und die Bedürfnisse des Unternehmens sind.

„2019 entwickelten wir zusammen mit Pfleiderer ein neues Messekonzept mit den Kernpunkten weniger Bauchladen, dafür mehr Konzentration auf Highlights sowie viel Raum für Begegnungen und Gespräche", so die Architektin.

Der Pfleiderer Messestand auf der Euroshop 2020 hatte den Arbeitstitel CATWALK, um das Thema Ladenbau intuitiv und emotional zu transportieren. Die beiden großflächigen, 6 Meter hohen Schaufenster-Fassaden lösen beim Besucher sofort Assoziationen zu Shops, Boutiquen und Einkaufsmeilen aus. In den Nischen stehen Schaufensterpuppen als Silhouetten in typischen Posen. Die Nischen selbst sind gefüllt mit Pfleiderer-Dekoren in horizontaler Anordnung, die auf diese Weise perspektivische Tiefe erzeugen. Das Thema Ladenbau wird auf der Standfläche wieder aufgenommen: Auf dem Auslagetisch präsentieren sich Holzwerkstoffmuster wie ikonische Waren – und transportieren so Messearchitektur mit Trend-Charakter.

EUROSHOP 2020 FOR PFLEIDERER

Continuous collaboration offers the opportunity to continue developing the trade fair design - sometimes building on one another step by step, sometimes in larger leaps or even breaks - depending on the development and needs of the company.

"In 2019, together with Pfleiderer, we developed a new trade fair concept with the main focus on fewer vendor trays, more focus on highlights and plenty of space for encounters and conversations," says the architect.

The Pfleiderer booth at Euroshop 2020 had the working title CATWALK in order to convey the topic of shopfitting intuitively and emotionally. The two large, 6-meter-high shop window facades immediately trigger associations with shops, boutiques and shopping streets in the visitor. In the niches there are mannequins as silhouettes in typical poses. The niches themselves are filled with Pfleiderer decors in a horizontal arrangement, which in this way create perspective depth. The topic of shopfitting is taken up again on the stand area: On the display table, wood-based material samples are presented like iconic goods - and thus transport trade fair architecture with a trend character.

CREATE
FUN**XT**IONAL
STYLES

XTREME
FUNCTION

XTREME
INSPIRATION

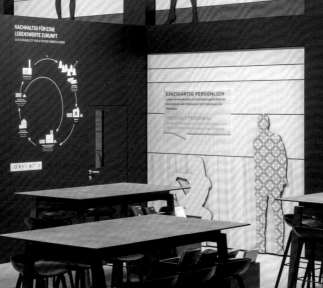

WERKSTOFFE WO___SED PANELS

ELEGANT UND
ALLTAGSTAUGLICH

NACHHALTIG FÜR EINE
LEBENSWERTE ZUKUNFT
SUSTAINABILITY FOR A FUTURE WORTH LIVING

EINZIGARTIG PERSÖNLICH

UNIQUELY PERSONAL

ENDS 2020

3S FRANKENMÖBELAUF DER MOW 2019

Der Messestand für 3S Frankenmöbel, Neukunde seit 2019, war eine echte Herausforderung - auf den ersten Blick schien der Messestand auf der MOW in Bad Salzuflen mit ca. 600 qm eher groß. „Als wir jedoch die Masse an zu zeigenden Möbeln mitgeteilt bekamen, wurde uns klar: zuerst musste ein ausgeklügeltes Konzept her", beschreibt die Architektin den Beginn der Zusammenarbeit.

Zusammen mit der Partneragentur kbw brands hat JÜRGENSARCHITEKTEN Gestaltungsmaximen entwickelt, um eine architektonisch durchgängige Linie ins kreative Chaos zu bringen: Definition der Standfläche durch Geschlossenheit, großzügige und einladende Eingangssituation mit Cafeteria, Schaffung eines durchgängigen gestalterischen Elements, welches außen und innen wahrnehmbar ist, klare Bewegungsflächen, ein definierter Rundgang über den Stand, Entwicklung eines durchgängigen Farbkonzepts sowie Orientierungssystems. Das Fazit: Der Kunde war sehr zufrieden mit dem Messestand, da die Produkte viel hochwertiger als in den Vorjahren präsentiert wurden. Auch in den Zahlen spiegelt sich der Erfolg wider: 3S Frankenmöbel erzielte 2019 mit dem neuen Messestand von JÜRGENSARCHITEKTEN einen Umsatzrekord auf der MOW.

3S FRANKENMÖBEL AT MOW 2019

The booth for 3S Frankenmöbel, a new customer since 2019, was a real challenge - at first glance the booth at the MOW in Bad Salzuflen seemed rather large at around 600 square meters. "However, when we were informed of the number of pieces of furniture to be displayed, it became clear to us that we had to come up with a sophisticated concept first," says the architect, describing the beginning of the collaboration.

Together with the partner agency kbw brands, JÜRGENSARCHITEKTEN has developed design maxims in order to bring an architecturally consistent line into creative chaos: definition of the stand space through unity, spacious and inviting entrance situation with cafeteria, creation of a consistent design element that is perceptible outside and inside, clear movement areas, a defined tour about the status, development of a consistent color concept and orientation system. The conclusion: The customer was very satisfied with the booth, as the products were presented in a much higher quality than in previous years. The success is also reflected in the numbers: 3S Frankenmöbel achieved a record turnover at the MOW in 2019 with the new JÜRGENSARCHITEKTEN exhibition stand.

SO VIELFÄLTIG WIE DAS LEBEN SELBST:
UNSERE STÜHLE FÜR JEDE GELEGENHEIT

UNSERE BETTEN
FÜR IHREN
TRAUMHAFTEN
START IN DEN TAG.

VARIANTE I
GEDREHTE KANTE

VARIANTE II
ABGESCHRAGTE KANTE

VARIANTE III
OVALE FORM

DAS TISCH-
SYSTEM
TI-0080:
IMMER DIE
PASSENDE
LÖSUNG.

BETTENSERIE
BE-0297

POLYTAN AUF DER FSB 2019

Polytan ist Hersteller von Sportböden aller Art, zu dessen Produktpalette auch Kunstrasen und Gymnastikbeläge gehören. JÜRGENSARCHITEKTEN betreut Polytan kontinuierlich seit 2013. Durchgängig in Sachen „Corporate Architecture" planten sie auch die Erweiterung des Firmensitzes in Burgheim. Die Messearchitektur für die FSB 2019 war von der räumlichen Gestaltung her puristisch angelegt– sie besteht aus einem langen schmalen Nebenraum-Kubus, der den optischen Rückhalt bildet und das Logo trägt. Die eigentliche Raumwirkung wird durch die Belegung der Flächen mit den Polytan-Produkten erzeugt.

„Durch die Gestaltung von Boden und Wand wird ein Kontinuum geschaffen, welches alle 2 Jahre wieder für überraschende Perspektiven sorgt. 2019 stand ganz im Zeichen der Nachhaltigkeits-Debatte, und so kreierte JÜRGENSARCHITEKTEN einen „grünen" Stand – im eigentlichen wie im übertragenen Sinne," erläutert Natalie Jürgens die Idee hinter dem Messekonzept.

POLYTAN AT FSB 2019

Polytan is manufacturer of all kinds of sports floors, whose product range also includes artificial turf and gymnastics surfaces. JÜRGENSARCHITEKTEN has been looking after Polytan continuously since 2013. In terms of corporate architecture, they also planned the expansion of the company headquarters in Burgheim. The exhibition architecture for FSB 2019 was purist in terms of the spatial design - it consists of a long, narrow cube of the adjoining room, which forms the visual support and bears the logo. The actual spatial effect is created by covering the surfaces with Polytan products.

"The design of the floor and wall creates a continuum that provides surprising perspectives every two years. 2019 was all about the sustainability debate, and so JÜRGENSARCHITEKTEN created a "green" stand - in the true and figurative sense," explains Natalie Jürgens the idea behind the trade fair concept.

KAUFFMANN THEILIG & PARTNER

Prof. Andreas Theilig, Rainer Lenz, Andrea Litterer, Thomas Theilig

KTP wurde 1988 von Andreas Theilig und Dieter Ben Kauffmann (bis 2019) als Kauffmann Theilig gegründet. Unter Kauffmann Theilig & Partner ergänzen Rainer Lenz (seit 1995), Manfred Ehrle (1999-2005) und Andrea Litterer und Thomas Theilig (seit 2018) die Büroführung als Partner. Als Freie Architekten PartGmbB, bzw. als KTP Generalplaner GmbH plant und realisiert das Büro im gesamten Hochbaubereich, sowie weltweit Messe- und Ausstellungsprojekte. Die umfassende Denk- und Arbeitsweise der Architekten erlaubt es, Bauherren bereits im Vorfeld in der Projektentwicklung zu unterstützen. Darüber hinaus pflegt das Büro eine intensive Zusammenarbeit mit Fachplanern aus der gesamten Hochbau- bzw. Messeplanung mit dem Ziel, ganzheitliche architektonische Lösungen in einem interdisziplinären Team zu entwickeln. Aus den spezifischen Bedingungen des Ortes und der Aufgabenstellung entwickelt KTP städtebauliche und architektonische Konzepte und betreut diese in allen Leistungsphasen von Planung bis Ausführung. Diese Konzepte berücksichtigen die Komplexität und Vielschichtigkeit aller Aspekte und schaffen gleichzeitig signifikante Bilder. Die Konzepte und Bauten wurden mit zahlreichen nationalen als auch internationalen Architektur und Designpreisen ausgezeichnet.

KTP was founded in 1988 by Andreas Theilig and Dieter Ben Kauffmann (until 2019) as Kauffmann Theilig. Under Kauffmann Theilig & Partner Rainer Lenz (since 1995), Manfred Ehrle (1999-2005) and Andrea Litterer and Thomas Theilig (since 2018) complement the office management as partners. As independent architects PartGmbB, respectively as KTP Generalplaner GmbH, the office plans and realizes in the entire building construction sector as well as worldwide fair and exhibition projects. The comprehensive way of thinking and working of the architects allows to support clients in the project development already in the run-up. In addition, the office cultivates intensive cooperation with specialist planners from the entire building construction and trade fair planning sector with the aim of developing holistic architectural solutions in an interdisciplinary team. Based on the specific conditions of the location and the task, KTP develops urban and architectural concepts and supervises them in all phases from planning to execution. These concepts consider the complexity and multilayeredness of all aspects and create significant images at the same time. The concepts and buildings have been awarded numerous national and international architecture and design prizes.

DAIMLER NUTZFAHRZEUGE AUF DER IAA HANNOVER 2018

In den Messehallen 14/15 wurde die Präsentation von Daimler Trucks auf der 67. IAA für Nutzfahrzeuge in Hannover neu gestaltet. Durch einen Intro-Tunnel mit Infotheke betraten die Besucher über eine erhöhte Plattform und Treppenanlagen das Standgeschehen und überblickten hierdurch das gesamte Spektrum der Marken Mercedes-Benz, Setra und Fuso. Der Mehrmarkenauftritt war gekennzeichnet durch eine Deckeninstallation aus topografisch gekrümmten Lamellen mit integrierten LED-Streifen. Die so medial bespielte Fläche setzte sich aus vier Teilflächen zu einem einheitlichen Raumgefüge zusammen, dessen Öffnung im Zentrum die Highlight-Fläche darunter betonte. Diese war Klammer und Treffpunkt und lieferte über den Rundumblick ein Verständnis über alle Themen der Marken. Den räumlichen Abschluss bildete eine zweigeteilte Markenwand: Rückgesetzte Nische schufen gezielte Bereiche für Nahkommunikation, bildeten Bezüge zu den Cateringbereichen und lieferten einen räumlichen Zusammenhang über die jeweiligen Marken hinweg. In die Markenwand integriert waren Medienflächen wie auch Leuchtkästen für die Kommunikation.

DAIMLER COMMERCIAL VEHICLES AT THE IAA HANNOVER 2018

In the exhibition halls 14/15, the presentation of Daimler Trucks at the 67th IAA for Commercial Vehicles in Hanover was redesigned. Through an intro tunnel with an information counter, visitors entered the booth via a raised platform and stairs and thus got an overview of the entire spectrum of the brands Mercedes-Benz, Setra and Fuso. The multi-brand presence was characterized by a ceiling installation made of topographically curved slats with integrated LED strips. The area covered by media was composed of four sub-areas to form a uniform spatial structure, the opening of which in the center emphasized the highlight area below. This was the bracket and meeting point and provided an understanding of all brand issues through the all-round view. The spatial conclusion was a two-part brand wall: recessed niches created targeted areas for close communication, created references to the catering areas and provided a spatial connection across the respective brands. Media areas and light boxes for communication were integrated into the brand wall.

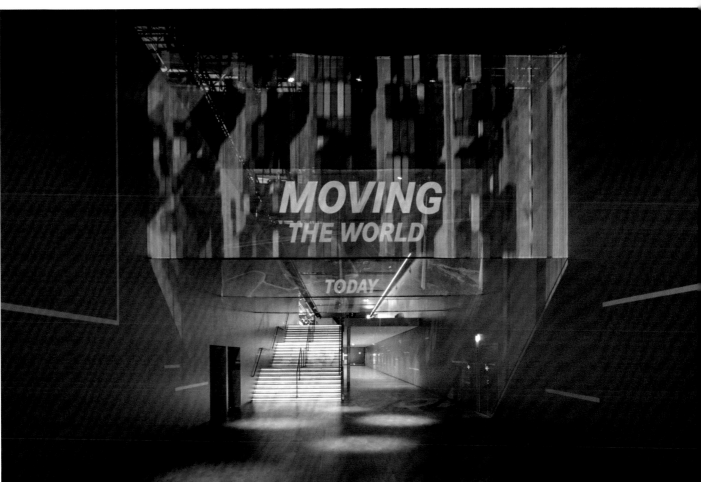

PERI AUF DER *BAUMA* MÜNCHEN 2019

PERI ist einer der größten Hersteller von Schalungs- und Gerüstsystemen weltweit. Für die Baumaschinenmesse bauma 2019 wurde der Messeauftritt der Firma neu gestaltet, mit dem Ziel eines flexiblen und wiedereinsetzbaren Messestandes. Für einen schnellen Aufbau und eine hohe Transluzenz entschied man sich für eine Leichtbauhalle mit Membran-Kissen. Die bedruckten Außenkissen dienten als Blickfang und waren dynamischer Auftakt. Die Innenkissen boten einen einheitlichen Hintergrund für die Exponate und beruhigten das Gesamtbild der Ausstellung. Die von der Halle baulich getrennte Ausstellung selbst war durch einen ovalen Luftraum geprägt, der von Rampe, Tribüne und Freitreppe gerahmt, einen zentralen Markplatz als Präsentationsfläche ausbildete. Die Besucher betraten die Ausstellung über die auf dem Gelände meist frequentierte Ecke, und wurden von dort über die Infotheke in einem Rundgang über das Obergeschoss um die Exponate und den Marktplatz herumgeleitet. Hierdurch waren alle Exponate dreidimensional erlebbar. Über dem Marktplatz bildete sich zudem eine Tribüne aus, von welcher sich die Präsentationsfläche auch im Sitzen beobachten ließ.

PERI AT *BAUMA* MUNICH 2019

PERI is one of the largest manufacturers of formwork and scaffolding systems worldwide. For the construction machinery trade fair bauma 2019, the company's trade fair presence was redesigned with the aim of a flexible and reusable booth. A lightweight hall with membrane cushions was chosen for quick assembly and high translucency. The printed outer cushions served as eye-catchers and were a dynamic start. The inner cushions provided a uniform background for the exhibits and calmed the overall picture of the exhibition. The exhibition itself, which is structurally separate from the hall, was characterized by an oval air space, which, framed by a ramp, grandstand and outside staircase, formed a central market square as a presentation area. The visitors entered the exhibition via the most frequented corner on the site, and from there they were guided around the exhibits and the market place via the information desk in a tour of the upper floor. This enabled all exhibits to be experienced in three dimensions. A grandstand also formed above the market square, from which the presentation area could also be watched while seated.

Ingenieurbau · Civil Engineering

MAIER + HOLLENBECK ARCHITEKTEN

Klaus Hollenbeck, Walter Maier

Gemeinsam blicken die Architekten Walter Maier und Klaus Hollenbeck auf über 60 Jahre Erfahrung zurück. In ihrem Büro vereinen sie Architekten, Fachplaner, Künstler, Grafiker und Szenografen und binden in einer interdisziplinären Arbeitsweise immer wieder auch fachfremde Akteure in Prozesse ein. Die Projekte reichen von der Ausstellungsgestaltung über die Nachnutzung kirchlicher Bauten bis hin zu Pflegeheimen und Kindertagesstätten. Themen wie Nachhaltiges Bauen, alternative Wohnkonzepte oder Stadtentwicklung sind fester Bestandteil sowohl der konzeptionellen, als auch der praktischen Arbeit bei Maier + Hollenbeck. Durch die inhaltliche Bandbreite und unterschiedlichste Größenordnungen der Projekte, werden klassische Denk- und Planungsprozesse aufgebrochen. „Denn nur die Offenheit des eigenen Denkens ermöglicht Architektur und Gestaltung von Relevanz."

Together, architects Walter Maier and Klaus Hollenbeck can look back on over 60 years of experience. In their office, they combine architects, specialist planners, artists, graphic designers and scenographers, and in an interdisciplinary way of working, they repeatedly involve actors from outside the field in processes. Their projects range from exhibition design and the re-use of church buildings to nursing homes and day-care centres. Topics such as sustainable building, alternative housing concepts or urban development are an integral part of both the conceptual and practical work at Maier + Hollenbeck. Due to the wide range of content and the different scales of the projects, classic thinking and planning processes are broken down. "Because only the openness of one's own thinking makes architecture and design of relevance possible."

PAPIERMUSEUM DÜREN

Als Gesamtkunstwerk aus Architektur, Gestaltung und Grafikdesign bietet das durch Hollenbeck Architektur umfassend sanierte und erweiterte Papiermuseum Düren, dem für die Papierstadt Düren so bedeutenden Werkstoff einen kraftvollen Ort der Auseinandersetzung.

Die Architektur ragt einer Papierskulptur gleich in den Himmel und folgt in ihrer Gestaltung drei Archetypen der Papierverarbeitung: Faltung, Wasserzeichen und Prägung. Dabei verbindet sie Fassade Bestands- und Neubau miteinander und verleiht dem Haus die Anmutung eines gänzlich neuen Bauwerks. Die ebenfalls durch Hollenbeck Architektur gestaltete Ausstellung atmet Papier, mit handgeschriebenen Texten, kunstfertigen Papiergrafiken und einem interaktiven Begleitbuch. Das Design reagiert dabei gleichermaßen auf das ausstellungsbestimmende Thema „Papier" und die Bedürfnisse blinder und sehbehinderter Menschen – ganz im Sinne der Stadt Düren, die sich neben ihrer Identität als Stadt des Papiers, auch als Stadt der Blinden versteht. Das Design setzt bedürfnisorientiert auf eine kontrastierende Gestaltung und lässt die Besucherinnen und Besucher sich innerhalb der bedruckten Seiten eines Buches wähnen.

PAPER MUSEUM DÜREN

As a synthesis of architecture, design and graphic design, the Paper Museum Düren, comprehensively renovated and expanded by Hollenbeck Architektur, offers the material so important to the paper city of Düren a powerful place for debate.

The architecture rises into the sky like a paper sculpture and follows three archetypes of paper processing in its design: folding, watermarking and embossing. The façade combines existing and new constructions, giving the building the appearance of a completely new structure. The exhibition, also designed by Hollenbeck Architektur, breathes paper, with handwritten texts, artful paper graphics and an interactive accompanying book. The design responds in equal measure to the exhibition's defining theme of "paper" and the needs of blind and visually impaired people, entirely in keeping with the spirit of the city of Düren, which sees itself not only as a city of paper, but also as a city of the blind. The design is based on a need-oriented contrasting design and allows visitors to imagine themselves within the printed pages of a book.

MUSEUM KARL-MARX-HAUS

Die neue Dauerausstellung des Museum Karl-Marx-Haus in Trier rückt den authentischen Ort ins Zentrum des gestalterischen Konzepts. Die Arbeitsgemeinschaft Hollenbeck Architektur / projekt2508 in Zusammenarbeit mit Lim und Freunden, macht das Geburtshaus des berühmten Denkers zum Exponat. Die Ausstellungsarchitektur unterstützt die Sichtbarkeit der Räume und greift, modern interpretiert, Elemente bürgerlichen Wohnens auf. Karl Marx drückte seine Gedanken aus indem er schrieb und so wird in der Ausstellung Schrift zum gestalterischen Stilmittel. Von Hand, direkt auf die Wände des Karl-Marx-Hauses aufgebracht, entwickelt sie eine eigenständige ästhetische Wirkung. Die Ausstellungsgestaltung überführt Gedankenkonstrukte in Exponate und macht diese intuitiv und erlebbar. Digitale und analoge Installationen visualisieren passgenau den Kern komplexer Sachverhalte und geben den Besucherinnen und Besuchern dennoch gedanklichen Freiraum, um die Bedeutung des intensiv diskutierten Karl Marx zu reflektieren.

KARL MARX HOUSE MUSEUM

The new permanent exhibition of the Museum Karl-Marx-Haus in Trier places the authentic location at the centre of the design concept. The consortium Hollenbeck Architektur / projekt2508 in cooperation with Mathias Lim und Freunden, turns the birthplace of the famous thinker into an exhibit. The exhibition architecture supports the visibility of the rooms and, with a modern interpretation, picks up on elements of bourgeois living. Karl Marx expressed his thoughts by writing, and so writing becomes a creative stylistic device in the exhibition. Applied by hand directly onto the walls of the Karl Marx House, it develops an independent aesthetic effect. The exhibition design transforms thought constructs into exhibits and makes them intuitive and tangible. Digital and analogue installations precisely visualise the core of complex issues and yet give visitors mental space to reflect on the significance of the intensely discussed Karl Marx.

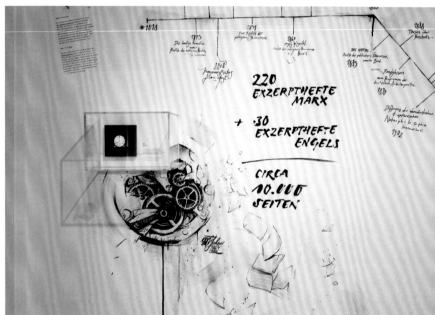

ERLEBNISAUFZUG BURG ALTENA

Der Erlebnisaufzug zur Burg Altena – das neue Tor zur Burg – stellt eine direkte und barrierefreie Verbindung von Burg und Innenstadt dar. Hollenbeck Architektur war für die komplexe Baumaßnahme von Tunnel und Aufzug verantwortlich und in einer Arbeitsgemeinschaft mit projekt2508 und Mathias Lim und Freunden darüber hinaus für die Ausstellung. Das gestalterische Leitmotiv setzt auf die Form des Tores. Sieben solcher Tore, multimedial als Ausstellungseinheiten inszeniert, rhythmisieren den rund 90 Meter in den Berg führenden Erlebnistunnel. 80 Meter nach oben fährt anschließend der eigentliche Erlebnisaufzug und entlässt seine Besucherinnen und Besucher auf den Burghof der Burg Altena. Ziel der Gestaltung ist es, ästhetischen Ansprüchen ebenso gerecht zu werden, wie den hohen Anforderungen an Technik und Brandschutz. Das Gesamtkonzept des Erlebnisaufzugs, das Architektur, Denkmalschutz, Tourismus und Edutainment verbindet, lässt die rund 900jährige Geschichte der Burg auf unterhaltsame Weise lebendig werden – Intuitiv und in einmaliger Atmosphäre.

ALTENA CASTLE EXPERIENCE LIFT

The adventure lift to Altena Castle, the new gateway to the castle, provides a direct and barrier-free connection between the castle and the town centre. Hollenbeck Architektur was responsible for the complex construction of the tunnel and lift and, in a joint venture with projekt2508 and Mathias Lim und Freunden, for the exhibition. The design leitmotif focuses on the form of the gate. Seven gates, staged as multimedia exhibition units, rhythmise the experience tunnel that leads some 90 m. into the mountain. The actual experience lift then travels 80 m. upwards and releases its visitors into the courtyard of Altena Castle. The aim of the design is to meet aesthetic requirements as well as the high demands on technology and fire protection. The overall concept of the adventure lift, which combines architecture, monument conservation, tourism and edutainment, brings the castle's 900-year history to life in an entertaining way, intuitively and in a unique atmosphere.

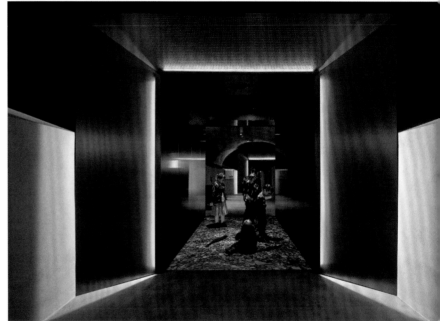

PRINZTRÄGER

Larissa Prinz & Marie Träger

PRINZTRÄGER entwickelt außergewöhnliche Konzepte für die Kommunikation im Raum. Die Diplom-Designerinnen Larissa Prinz und Marie Träger sind 2012 als Duo gestartet und betreuen inzwischen mit ihrem wachsenden Team Szenografie- und Designprojekte in ganz Deutschland. Für Auftraggeber aus Wirtschaft und Kultur beschäftigt sich das Designstudio mit dem Medium Raum und seinem narrativen Potential unter anderem in Ausstellungen und urbanen Inszenierungen. Weitere Schwerpunkte der Konzeptionsarbeit sind die Entwicklung von Brand Spaces und die Gestaltung und Planung der Arbeitswelten von morgen. Das Team mit Wurzeln in Kommunikationsdesign, Szenografie und Innenarchitektur begleitet seine Kunden durch räumliche Transformationsprozesse und gestaltet für kulturelle Institutionen ebenso wie für Start-Ups und internationale Player.

PRINZTRÄGER develops extraordinary concepts for communication in space. The graduate designers Larissa Prinz and MarieTräger started in 2012 as a duo and now manage scenography and design projects all over Germany with their growing team. For clients from business and culture, the design studio deals with the medium of space and its narrative potential, including exhibitions and urban staging. Further focal points of their conceptual work are the development of brandspaces and the design and planning of the tomorrow's working environments. The team with its roots in communication design, scenography and interior design accompanies its customers through spatial transformation processes and designs for cultural institutions as well as for start-ups and international players.

VONOVIA – 100 JAHRE WOHNGESCHICHTE

100 Jahre Wohngeschichte in Deutschland beleuchtet die gleichnamige Ausstellung in der Bochumer Unternehmenszentrale von Vonovia. Historische Chroniken aus dem Unternehmensarchiv, bunte Kachelkreationen aus Badmodernisierungen der 70er Jahre und Einblicke in die Zukunft des modularen Bauens – dies und vieles mehr verbindet ein langer Zeitstrahl durch das Gebäude zu einer spannenden Ausstellungssituation. Auf das besondere, nicht museale Setting eines langen, lichtdurchfluteten Durchgangsraumes wurde durch das Designteam szenografisch reagiert: mit einem Entwurf, der die weitläufigen Blickachsen nicht zustellt und intelligent Fläche für die Ausstellungsinhalte generiert. So ist eine charmante und unprätentiöse Ausstellungssituation entstanden, die die wechselvolle Unternehmensgeschichte des Immobilienkonzerns anhand von Milestones ebenso kurzweilig wie reflektiert und informativ aufbereitet.

VONOVIA – 100 YEARS OF LIVING HISTORY

100 years of residential history in Germany are explored by an exhibition of the same name at the Vonovia company headquarters in Bochum. Historical chronicles from the company´s archive, colorful tile creations from bathroom modernisations of the 1970´s and insights into the future of modular building – this and much more is combined in a long timeline through the building to create an exciting exhibition. The design team responded scenographically to the special, non-museal setting of a long, light-flooded passage space: with a design that does not obstruct the wide viewing axes, but intelligently generates space for the exhibition's content. This has created a charming and unpretentious exhibition situation that reflects and informatively prepares the entire corporate history of the real estate group on the basis of milestones.

ZECHE ZOLLERN - REVIERGESTALTEN

Die große Sonderausstellung „RevierGestalten – von Orten und Menschen" im LWL Industriemuseum Zeche Zollern in Dortmund zeigte 2018 auf über 600 qm Ausstellungsfläche den Wandel des Ruhrgebiets rund um den Nieder-gang des Steinkohlebergbaus. Die Besucher*innen stöberten durch verlassene Zechen, erlebten urbane Teilhabe gestern und heute und tauchten dank Videoinstallationen mit Zeitzeugeninterviews in die Familiengeschichten ehemaliger Bergleute ein. Altvertrautes aus der Lebenswelt des Kohlenpotts wie eine „Bude", die interaktive Aus-stellungsinhalte, aber – natürlich! – auch „Bömsken" bereit hielt, begegneten den Gästen ebenso wie Sitzland-schaften aus Europaletten als Symbol der urbanen Teilhabe. In enger Zusammenarbeit mit den Fachleuten des Kurator*innenteams ist in der historischen Zechenwerkstatt ein innovatives, multimedial ausformuliertes und parti-zipatives Ausstellungserlebnis entstanden – mit Mut zu vielen Hands-On-Konzepten und dem einen oder anderen Augenzwinkern.

ZECHE ZOLLERN – REVIERGESTALTEN

The large special exhibition "RevierGestalten - von Orten und Menschen" ("Ruhr district, places and people") at the LWL Industriemuseum Zeche Zollern in Dortmund in 2018 showed the transformation of the Ruhr area around the decline of hard coal mining on more than 600 square meters of exhibition space. Visitors rummaged through abandoned coal mines, experienced urban participation and, thanks to video installations with interviews with con-temporary witnesses, immersed themselves in the family stories of former miners. Old but familiar things from the habitat of the coal pot like a "shack, containing interactive exhibition contents as well as – of course! – "Bömsken" (regional word for candy), met the guests as well as seating landscapes made of europallets as a symbol of urban participation. In close cooperation with the experts of the curator team, an innovative, multi-media and participa-tory exhibition experience has been created in the historic coal mining/colliery workshop with many hands-on concepts and a subtle wink.

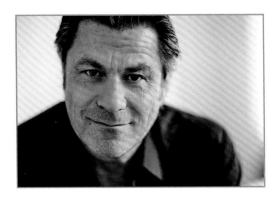

QUADT INTERIOR ARCHITECTURE

Werner Quadt

QUADT INTERIOR ARCHITECTURE, gegründet 1994 in Köln, verfügt über eine 26 jährige Erfahrung in den unterschiedlichsten Disziplinen der Customer Journey.

Wir entwickeln Raumkonzepte für den europäischen Einrichtungshandel auf Flächen bis zu 40.000 qm, die sämtliche Aspekte von Architektur, Innenarchitektur, Marketing und Kommunikation vereinen. Im Mittelpunkt unserer Arbeit steht die ganzheitliche Entwicklung von marken – und zielgruppengerechten Stores mit individuellem Charakter und unverwechselbarer Identität. Dabei achten wir in unseren Konzeptionen auf die Integration von High Tech und High Touch. Die Ausstellung wird zur Bühne für Besucher, Produkte und Ereignisse, sie muss ebenso rationalen wie emotionalen, aber auch optischen wie technischen Ansprüchen gerecht werden. Mit über 500 realisierten Projekten, weit mehr als 1,5 Millionen QM erstellter Store Fläche und zahlreichen Veröffentlichungen in der Fachpresse zählt das Büro zu den renommiertesten Planern im Einrichtungshandel.

QUADT INTERIOR ARCHITECTURE, founded in Cologne in 1994, has 26 years of experience in the most diverse disciplines of customer journey.

We develop interior concepts for the European furniture trade on areas of up to 40.000 m², combining all aspects of architecture, interior design, marketing and communication. Our work focuses on the holistic development of brand and target group-oriented stores with individual character and unmistakable identity. We pay attention to the integration of high tech and high touch. The exhibition becomes a stage for visitors, products and events. It has to meet rational and emotional as well as visual and technical demands. With over 500 completed projects, well over 1.5 million QM of store space created and numerous publications in the trade press, the office is one of the most renowned planners in the furniture trade.

DE RUCCI BEDDING GERMANY, KÖLN

Das Projekt de Rucci Bedding Germany in Köln war der erste Flagship – Store des chinesischen Konzerns in Europa und diente als Vorbild für weitere Stores. Das nach Kriegsende vom populären Kölner Architekten Wilhelm Riphan entworfene Gebäude steht unter Denkmalschutz und repräsentiert mit seiner damaligen modernen Form maßgeblich den Wiederaufbau der zerstörten Stadt. Der Innenausbau der 1000 Quadratmeter großen Ausstellung erstreckt sich über drei Etagen, stilgebende Elemente wie die seinerzeit typischen Glasvitrinen bzw. Eingänge wurden bei der Innenraumgestaltung bzw. Fassadengestaltung aufgegriffen und neu interpretiert.

DE RUCCI BEDDING GERMANY, COLOGNE

The de Rucci Bedding Germany project in Cologne was the Chinese group's first flagship store in Europe and served as a model for other stores. The building, designed after the end of the war by the popular Cologne architect Wilhelm Riphan, is a listed building and with its then modern form represents the reconstruction of the destroyed city. The interior design of the 1.000 m² exhibition extends over three floors. Stylistic elements such as the glass showcases and entrances typical of the time were taken up and reinterpreted in the interior design and façade design.

SCHMALENBACH DESIGN, NORDHORN

Ästhetik mit System, dafür steht die Manufaktur Schmalenbach Design aus Gummersbach. In Kooperation mit diesem innovativen Möbelhersteller haben wir einen 300 qm großen Showroom beim Küchenhändler Ekelhoff in Nordhorn gestaltet.

Die Ausstellung besticht durch ein puristisches und zeitloses Design und zeigt die Vielfalt an eleganten Möglichkeiten und ausgereiften Funktionen, die Schmalenbach Design in Perfektion zu bieten hat.

SCHMALENBACH DESIGN, NORDHORN

Aesthetics with system, that's what the Schmalenbach Design manufactory from Gummersbach stands for. In cooperation with this innovative furniture manufacturer, we have designed a 300 m² showroom at kitchen dealer Ekelhoff in Nordhorn.

The showroom impresses with its purist and timeless design and shows the variety of elegant possibilities and sophisticated functions that Schmalenbach Design has to offer in perfection.

WÜRTHNER WOHNEN, VILLINGEN – SCHWENNINGEN

Die Firma Würthner Wohnen in Villingen – Schwenningen präsentiert auf 3.000 qm Ausstellungsfläche eine Zusammenstellung harmonischer Einrichtungen. Im Showroom findet man Inspirationen für einen ganz individuellen Einrichtungsstil. Die Kombination von Solitärmöbeln, internationalen Marken – Highlights sowie aktuellen Trends machen die Ausstellung zu einer ersten Adresse in der Region.

WÜRTHNER WOHNEN, VILLINGEN - SCHWENNINGEN

The company Würthner Wohnen in Villinge, Schwenningen presents a compilation of harmonious furnishings on 3.000 m² of exhibition space. In the showroom you will find inspirations for a very individual furnishing style. The combination of solitary furniture, international brands and highlights as well as current trends make the exhibition a first address in the region.

RANGER DESIGN

Kurt Ranger

Hinter diesem Namen steht ein Team um den Designer Kurt Ranger: Spezialisten aus den Bereichen Konzeption, Innenarchitektur, Szenografie, Grafikdesign, Produktdesign und Mediendesign erarbeiten kreative Ausstellungen, Markenwelten, Museen, Messestände und Showrooms. Die Fähigkeit, Inhalte und Botschaften zu entwickeln, daraus konzeptionell schlüssige, erzählerische Handlungsabläufe zu entwickeln, in atmosphärische Bilder zu übersetzen und dabei die Exponate „zum Sprechen zu bringen" findet sehr positive Resonanz. Innovative Gestaltungsansätze, Budgettreue und professionelle Abwicklung von Projekten bis ins Detail sind eine weitere Stärke. Mit der Gestaltung von über 130 Ausstellungs- und Museumsprojekten hat das Team sehr viele Erfahrungen mit der Vermittlung von komplexen Inhalten gesammelt. Klare inhaltliche Strukturen, der Mix aus verschiedenen Darstellungsformen, der vernetzte Einsatz von Medien, Rhythmus und Spannung der Dramaturgie sind wesentliche Elemente der Gestaltung. Ranger Design vertritt die Auffassung, dass Auftraggeber, Experten und Gestalter als Team im Dialog arbeiten müssen, um ein optimales Ergebnis zu entwickeln. Mehrere Auszeichnungen für Designqualität und vernetzte Medienkonzepte dokumentieren den Erfolg dieser Vorgehensweise.

Behind this name stands a team around the designer Kurt Ranger: specialists in conception, interior design, scenography, graphic design, product design and media design, creative exhibitions, brand worlds, museums, exhibition stands and showrooms. The ability to develop content and messages, to develop conceptually coherent, narrative sequences of action, to translate them into atmospheric images and, the exhibits have met with a very positive response. Innovative design approaches, budget compliance and professional handling of projects down to the last detail are further strengths. With the design of over 130 exhibition and museum projects, the team has gained a great deal of experience in conveying complex content. Clear content structures, the mix of different forms of presentation, the networked use of media, rhythm and tension of the dramaturgy are essential elements of design. Ranger Design is of the opinion that clients, experts and designers must work as a team in dialogue in order to develop an optimal result. Several awards for design quality and networked media concepts document the success of this approach.

FC BAYERN MUSEUM

Als ein Ort der Emotionen und der Identität zeigt das FC Bayern Museum in der Allianz Arena in München die Erfolgsgeschichte des Vereins seit dessen Gründung im Jahr 1900. Auf 3.000 qm Fläche konzipierte und plante Ranger Design die interaktive Präsentation. Zeiträume erzählen Geschichte mit Geschichten, in der Hall of Fame werden große Fußballpersönlichkeiten präsentiert. Fankultur, die aktuelle Mannschaft, ein Spielbereich und Themeninseln zeigen „die Seele des Vereins". Aktuelle Sonderausstellungen ergänzen die ständige Schau, die laufend aktualisiert wird. Das FC Bayern Museum etablierte sich mit über 350.000 Besuchern im Jahr unter den fünf erfolgreichsten Museen in München. Der Rat für Formgebung nominierte und zeichnete 2020 das FC Bayern Museum für „Excellent Architecture" als Winner aus. Bereits 2013 war das FC Bayern Museum mit dem Sinus Integration Award ausgezeichnet worden.

FC BAYERN MUSEUM

As a place of emotions and identity, the FC Bayern Museum in the Allianz Arena in Munich shows the club's success story since its foundation in 1900. 3.000 m² of space were used by Ranger Design to conceive and plan the interactive presentation. Time periods tell history with stories in the Hall of Fame. Fan culture, the current team, a game area and theme islands show the soul of the club. Current special exhibitions complement the permanent show, which is constantly updated. With over 350.000 visitors a year, the FC Bayern Museum has established itself as one of the five most successful museums in Munich. In 2020, the German Design Council nominated and awarded winner the FC Bayern Museum for "Excellent Architecture". In 2013, the FC Bayern Museum had received the Sinus Integration Award.

HILTI – OUR INNOVATION CULTURE

In enger Zusammenarbeit mit Hilti entwickelte Ranger Design eine Konzeption, die das Thema „Innovation by Hilti" in den Mittelpunkt stellt. Interaktive Ausstellungsmodule zeigen, wie grundlegende Fragestellungen zu Ideen, Entwicklungen und neuen Produkten führen und dokumentieren Methoden und Lösungswege der Entwickler. An einem langen Touchscreen-Tisch werden Ideen und Entwicklungsprozesse sichtbar gemacht und Kreativmethoden, systematische Planungsschritte, Einflussfaktoren und Produktentwicklungen thematisiert. Filmeinblendungen ergänzen die Entwicklungslinien. Mitarbeiterinnen und Mitarbeiter führen in einem interaktiven, teils virtuellen, teils gefilmten Rundgang durch das neue Innovationszentrum. Am Anfang der Ausstellung steht ein Handmeißel der Bronzezeit, eine über 3.000 Jahre alte Entwicklung. An diesem Beispiel wird erklärt, wie selbstverständlich erscheinende und altbekannte Produkte erhebliches Potential beinhalten können: Hilti entwickelte einen sich selbst nachschärfenden Meißel.

HILTI – OUR INNOVATION CULTURE

In close cooperation with Hilti, Ranger Design developed a concept that focuses on the theme "Innovation by Hilti". Interactive exhibition modules show how fundamental questions lead to ideas, developments and new products and document methods and solutions designed by the developers. Ideas are made visible at a long touch-screen table and creative methods, systematic planning steps, influencing factors and product designs are discussed. Film insertions complement the lines. Employees lead an interactive, partly virtual, partly filmed tour through the new innovation center. The exhibition begins with a chisel from the Bronze Age, a development that is over 3.000 years old. This example is used to explain how seemingly self-evident and well-known products can contain considerable potential: Hilti developed a self-sharpening chisel.

How does Hilti define innovation?

Wie definiert Hilti Innovation?

How can we reduce vibration?

Was können wir Vibrationen reduzieren?

Our Roots

Welcome
Great to have you here!

OSRAM WORLD OF LIGHT

Ranger Design war mit der Konzeption, Planung und Gestaltung einer Ausstellung beauftragt worden und setzte das Projekt als Generalplaner und -übernehmer um. Auf 1.300 qm Fläche entstand ein multifunktionaler Showroom, der Osram als neuen Hightech-Konzern zeigt. Die World of Light ist Arbeitsraum und eine hochflexible Bühne für die Präsentation des Unternehmens, seiner Werte, seiner Innovationen und seiner Kompetenz rund um das Thema Licht. Die Osram World of Light wendet sich mit zielgruppenorientierter Kommunikation an die hauptsächlichen Besuchergruppen: Kunden, Partner, Investoren und Analysten, Journalisten, Bewerber sowie die Mitarbeiter von Osram. Sie wurde vom Rat für Formgebung mit dem German Design Award 2020 für „Excellent Architecture" und mit dem Sinus Integration Award 2020 der Messe Frankfurt ausgezeichnet.

OSRAM WORLD OF LIGHT

Ranger Design was commissioned with the concept, planning and design of an exhibition and implemented the project as general planner and contractor. A multi-functional showroom was created on 1.300 m² of floor space, showing Osram as a new high-tech group. The World of Light is a working space and a highly flexible stage for presenting the company, its values, its innovations and its expertise in the field of lighting. Osram World of Light addresses the main groups of visitors with target group-oriented communication: customers, partners, investors and analysts, journalists, applicants and Osram employees. It was awarded by the German Design Award 2020 by the German Design Council for Excellent Architecture and the Sinus Integration Award 2020 by Messe Frankfurt.

HÖRMANN FORUM

Das Hörmann Forum in Steinhagen, das Ausstellungs- und Schulungszentrum des Marktführers für Türen, Tore und Antriebstechnik informiert über alle Produktbereiche von Hörmann. Parallel zur Entwicklung des Gebäudes wurde die Ausstellung durch Ranger Design entwickelt, um eine optimale Synthese von Gebäude und Inhalt zu erreichen. Die Geschichte des Familienunternehmens, seine Werte und die Unternehmenskultur sind Teil der innovativen Ausstellung. Industrietore, Garagentore, Spezialtüren, Brandschutztüren, Haustüren, Antriebe und Steuerungstechnik werden präsentiert. Klare Strukturen und interaktive Informationselemente führen durch die Produktgattungen. Touchscreens an allen Produkten ermöglichen mehrsprachige und interaktive Kommunikation mit verschiedenen Besuchergruppen. Hörmann präsentiert sich als weltweit aufgestelltes Familienunternehmen in der 3. und 4. Generation. Die Ausstellung kommuniziert über die Produktpräsentation hinaus auch tiefergehende Informationen zu Qualität, Sicherheit und innovativer Architektur mit Türen und Toren.

HÖRMANN FORUM

The Hörmann Forum in Steinhagen, the exhibition and training centre of the market leader for doors, gates and operator technology provides information on all company´s product areas. Parallel to the development of the building, the exhibition was developed by Ranger Design to achieve an optimum synthesis of building and content. The history of the family business, its values and corporate culture are part of the innovative exhibition. Industrial doors, garage doors, special doors, fire doors, entrance doors, drives and control technology are presented. Clear structures and interactive information elements lead through the product categories. Touch screens on all products allow multilingual and interactive communication with different groups of visitors. Hörmann presents itself as a globally positioned family business in the 3rd and 4th generation. In addition to the product presentation, the exhibition also communicates in-depth information on quality, safety and innovative architecture with doors and gates.

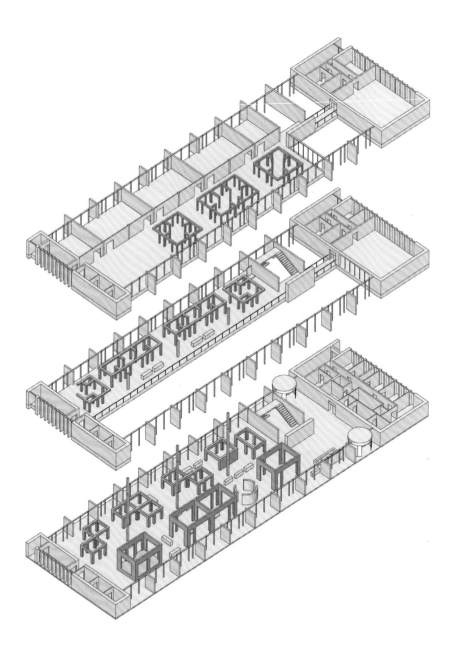

RAUMKONTOR INNENARCHITEKTUR

Dipl. Ing. Andrea Weitz & Prof. Jens Wendland

raumkontor ist ein transdisziplinäres Team von Innenarchitekten, Architekten und Mediengestaltern, das 1993 von Andrea Weitz und Jens Wendland gegründet wurde. Im Zusammenwirken von Architektur, Innenarchitektur und Design entwickelt das Büro ganzheitliche Raumkonzepte. Raum zu planen bedeutet für die Entwerfer das Bündeln verschiedene Energiefelder (Funktionalitäten, Atmosphären, Handlungsstrategien, Kommunikationsimpulse, Farbe, Licht, Material und Form) zu einer erlebbar werdenden Identität. raumkontor entwickelt bei jedem Projekt auf den Auftraggeber und die Projektsituation zugeschnittene eigenständige Gestaltungslösungen. Klare und markante Leitideen und innovative funktionale Strukturen gewährleisten langfristig und nachhaltig Projektqualität. Das Büro ist für die Eigenständigkeit seiner Konzepte bekannt, die mehrfach mit Preisen bedacht wurden (Finest Interior Award, Famab Award, DDC, Iconic Award, German Design Award). raumkontor steht für das Andere in den Räumen und den Dingen, für die wesentliche Abweichung, die Charakter erzeugt. Das wird am Leitmotiv des Büros deutlich, das die Arbeit des Teams prägt: „Wir sind Gestalter. Durch uns werden die Dinge anders."

raumkontor is a transdisciplinary team of interior designers, architects and media designers founded in 1993 by Andrea Weitz and Jens Wendland. The office develops holistic spatial concepts in the interaction of architecture, interiors and design. For the designers, planning space means bundling various energy fields (functionalities, atmospheres, action strategies, communication impulses, colour, light, material and form) to create an identity that can be experienced. For each project, raumkontor develops independent design solutions tailored to the client and the project situation. Clear and distinctive guiding ideas and innovative functional structures guarantee long-term and sustainable project quality. The office is known for the independence of its concepts, which have been awarded several prizes (Finest Interior Award, Famab Award, DDC, Iconic Award, German Design Award). raumkontor stands for the other in rooms and things, for the essential deviation that creates character. This becomes clear from the leitmotif of the office, which shapes the work of the team: "we are designers. Through us things become different".

‚DER KLANG DER TAPETE‘
DEUTSCHES TAPETEN-INSTITUT, IMM 2015, KÖLN

Tapeten charakterisieren Räume nicht nur optisch – sie rufen auch akustische Assoziationen hervor, die von Mensch zu Mensch unterschiedlich sein können. Sie eröffnen einen Klangkosmos, erzeugen bestimmte Raumatmosphären und wecken Erinnerungen. Hier knüpft die Konzeption an. Der Messestand ist voller Besucher - aber zu sehen sind nur ihre Beine und Füße. Der Rest des Körpers verschwindet in großen begehbaren Zylindern, die von der Hallendecke hängen. Der erste Blick verrät nicht, was sich im Inneren verbirgt. Betritt man nun diese Röhrenwelt, so erlebt man ein wundersames Geschehen. Das Innere der schwarzen Tonnen ist jeweils in einem anderen Design gestaltet. Tapete umgibt einen von allen Seiten, expressiv und farbenfroh. Über das visuelle Erleben hinaus, erfahren die Besucher ein sinnliches Surround- Erlebnis: jede Tapete hat ihren eigenen Klangwelt, ihre eigene Klang- Story, die die Kraft der Tapete erlebbar werden lässt.

"THE SOUND OF WALLPAPER"
GERMAN WALLPAPER INSTITUTE, IMM 2015, COLOGNE

Wallpapers characterize rooms not only visually, they also evoke acoustic associations that can vary from person to person. They open up a sound cosmos, create certain room atmospheres and awaken memories. This is where the concept comes in. The exhibition stand is full of visitors - but all you can see are their legs. The rest of the body disappears into accessible cylinders hanging from the hall ceiling. At first glance it does not reveal what is hidden inside. If you now enter this world of tubes, you will experience a wondrous event. The interior of the black barrels is designed differently in each case. Wallpaper surrounds you from all sides, expressive and colourful. Beyond the visual experience, the visitors feel a sensual surround experience: each wallpaper has its own sound world, its own sound story, which makes the power of wallpaper tangible.

,CHROMATIC'
JUNG, POP-UP-INSTALLATION,
MILAN DESIGN WEEK, 2019

Schwarztönender Raum. Dann: Berührung. Dann: zi-
schender Atemhauch, schmelzender Silberhagel, Ne-
belpuls. Chromgeister erobern den Raum, Blitzlettern
tanzen Cha- Cha- Cha. Chromatic ist Energie, ist Dynamik, ist Leuchten. Alles ist möglich. Nichts passiert
ohne die Besucher. Zauber des Moments, Gunst des
Augenblicks, phantastische Reise. ,Chromatic' lautete
der Titel der JUNG Ausstellung im Rahmen der Milan
Design Week 2019. Das raumkünstlerische Experiment
verlieh der Innovationskraft des Herstellers von zu-
kunftssicherer Gebäudetechnik und ästhetischem Design eine Bühne, auf der Purismus und Chrom mit dem
Feinsinn der Le Corbusier- Farbwelten zusammenfand.
Die temporäre Installation erstreckte sich über die Räume einer Ballettschule in Mitten von Brera. Die Vielfalt
und Vielschichtigkeit der Inszenierung verknüpfte die
bis heute anhaltende architektonische Kraft der Jung-
Schalterikonen mit der Leichtigkeit eines multioptiona-
len Lebensgefühls und ließ das Staunen als Ausgangspunkt unseres Welterlebens wieder lebendig werden.

"CHROMATIC"
JUNG, POP-UP INSTALLATION,
MILAN DESIGN WEEK, 2019

Black-tinted room. Then: touch. Then: hissing breath,
melting silver hail, fog pulse. Chrome spirits conquer
space, lightning bolts dance Cha-Cha- Cha. Chromatic
is energy, is dynamics, is glow. Everything is possible.
Nothing happens without the visitors. Magic of the moment, favour of the moment, fantastic journey. "Chromatic" was the title of the JUNG exhibition as part of
Milan Design Week 2019. The spatial artistic experiment
gave the innovative strength of the manufacturer of fu-
ture-proof building technology and aesthetic design a
stage on which purism and chrome came together with
the subtlety of Le Corbusier's colour worlds. The temporary installation extended over the rooms of a ballet
school in the centre of Brera. The diversity and complexity of the production combined the architectural
power of the young switch icons, which is still enduring
today, with the lightness of a multi-optional attitude to
life and lie brought back to life the astonishment as the
starting point of our experience of the world.

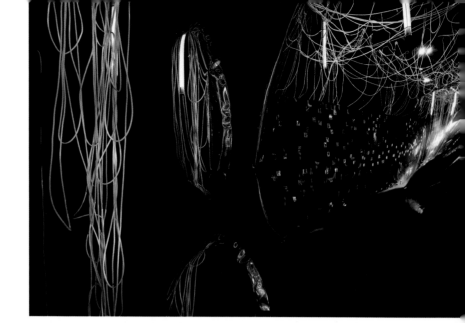

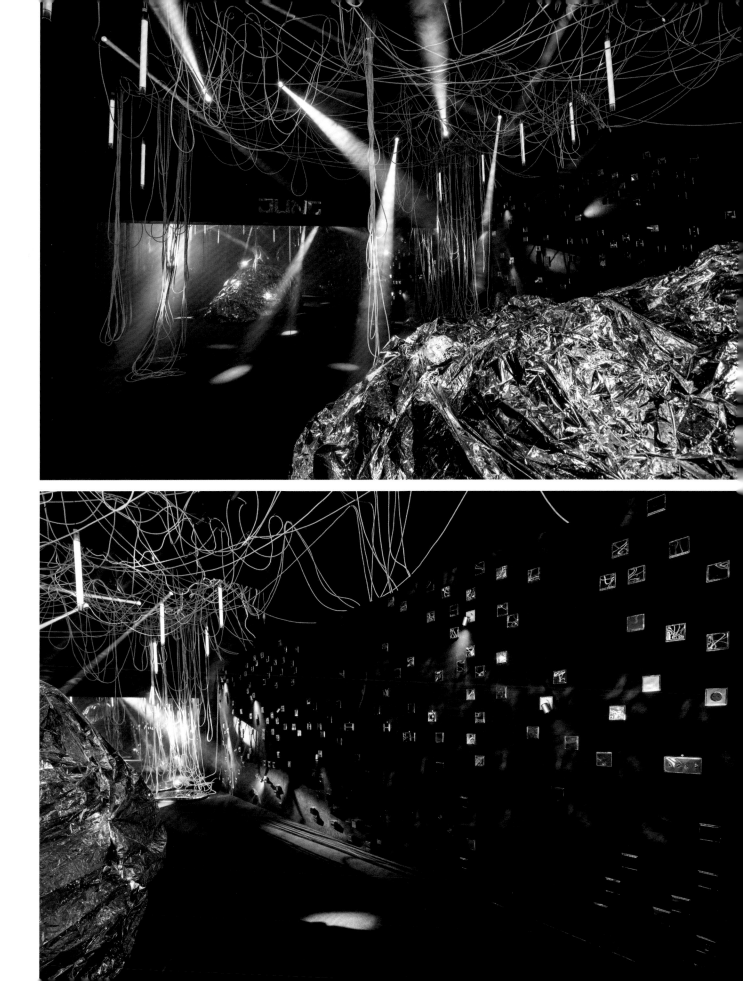

DIE WELT ALS BÜHNE
CARPET CONCEPT, ORGATEC 2018

Messen sind Orte voller visueller und akustischer Tur-
bulenzen: jeder versucht aufzufallen, einer den anderen
zu übertrumpfen. Um in diesem Kontext prägnant und
erinnerbar aufzutreten bedarf es daher einer besonde-
ren Strategie: Eine imposante, dynamisch abgewinkelte
hohe schwarze Wand lässt einen ‚Bühnenraum' entstehen, in dem die Produkte in Ihrer vielseitigen Materiali-
tät brillant zur Geltung kommen. Konsequenter Weise
imaginiert die Rückseite dieser Installation den typischen Eindruck eines Backstage- Szenarios. Hinter der
schwarzen Wand verbergen sich zweigeschossig Son-
derausstellungs- und Beratungsräume und die Stand-
gastronomie. Diese Räume sind durch eine intensive
Farbigkeit geprägt. Das Farbleuchten ist durch schlan-
ke Wandausschnitte von überall aus mehr zu erahnen
als zu sehen. Neben der gezielten Aufhellung einzelner
Exponate bleibt eine eindrucksvolle Installation aus
transluzenten leuchtenden Kreisen in Erinnerung, die
den Luftraum über dem langen Kommunikationstisch
akzentuiert. Die Konzeption zeigt, dass eine bewusste
Zurückhaltung im Formrepertoire den Blick wieder auf
das Eigentliche fokussieren kann: das Produkt und die
Menschen im Gespräch darüber.

THE WORLD AS A STAGE
CARPET CONCEPT, ORGATEC 2018

Trade fairs are places full of visual and acoustic turbu-
lence: everyone tries to stand out, one tries to outdo
the other. In order to appear in this context concisely
and memorably, a special strategy is therefore required:
an impressive, dynamically angled high black wall creates a space in which the products are brilliantly shown
to advantage in their versatile materiality. Consequent-
ly, the back of this installation imagines the typical
impression of a backstage scenario. Behind the black
wall are two-storey special exhibition and consultation
rooms and the stand catering. These rooms are characterised by an intensive colourfulness. Thanks to the
slim wall cut-outs, the coloured light can be seen rather
than guessed from everywhere. In addition to the targeted illumination of individual exhibits, an impressive
installation of translucent luminous circles, which ac-
centuates the air space above the long communication
table, remains in the memory. The concept shows that
a deliberate restraint in the repertoire of forms can re-
focus the view on the real thing: the product and the
people talking about it.

'GEWEBE XXL'
CAMIRA FABRICS LTD, ORGATEC 2018,
KÖLN

Messestände sind Orte, an denen ein Thema mit großer
Intensität erlebbar wird, sinnlich, überraschend, ein we-
nig verrückt vielleicht, auf jeden Fall aber einprägsam
und erinnerbar.

Dieses Credo stand am Anfang des Entwurfsprozesses
des Messestands für die Orgatec 2018, verbunden mit
der Frage danach, was denn den Kern der Produkte bildet, die camira herstellt. Es geht um Kette und Schuss,
um Fäden in wundervollen, leuchtenden Farben. Es
geht um die Gewebe, die camira in unterschiedlichsten Strukturen und aus verschiedensten Materialien
fertigt. Und das Ganze in einem Farbkanon, der den
Besuchern in Erinnerung bleiben wird: Feurige Rottö-
ne, sanfte Orange- Varianten, ein paar Spritzer Violett,
‚abgeschmeckt' mit der ganz in Schwarz gehaltenen
Standmöblierung, wie grob gemahlener Pfeffer auf einer köstlichen Mahlzeit. Der ganze Stand lebt, er atmet,
er repräsentiert mit jeder Faser einen zentralen Claim
des Unternehmens: Wir sind camira. Wir weben Stoffe!

"FABRIC XXL"
CAMIRA FABRICS LTD, ORGATEC 2018,
COLOGNE

Exhibition stands are places where a theme can be experienced with intensity, sensually, surprisingly, in a little crazy way perhaps, but in any case, memorable.

This credo was the starting point for the design process
of the trade fair stand for Orgatec 2018, combined with
the question as to what forms the core of the products
that camira manufactures. It's about warp and weft,
about threads in wonderful, bright colours. It's about
the fabrics that camira produces in the most diverse
structures and materials. And all of this in a canon of
colours that visitors will remember: fiery shades of
red, soft orange variants, a few splashes of violet, 'sea-
soned' with the stand furniture, which is entirely black,
like coarsely ground pepper on a delicious meal. The
whole stand lives, it breathes, and with every fibre it
represents a central claim of the company: We are
Camira. We weave fabrics!

SONS. AGENTUR FÜR STRATEGISCHE UND KREATIVE MARKENENTWICKLUNG

Thomas Stricker, Till Hamm, Markus Müller-Kempf

In der dritten Dimension haben Marken die Chance, mehr zu zeigen als ihren Namen und das Logo: ihre Persönlichkeit, die Welt in der sie zuhause sind und wofür sie stehen.

Wir denken, fühlen und handeln 360° Grad. Arbeiten ganzheitlich und interdisziplinär. Übersetzen aufmerksamkeitsstarke Ideen bei Bedarf auch in Corporate Architecture. Das lässt uns Erlebnisse im Raum schaffen, die Marken eine besondere Strahlkraft verleihen. Die begeistern und Vertrauen wecken, weil sie starke Identifikation und langfristige Bindung fördern. Und die eben Marken eine nachhaltige Bühne geben, damit diese glänzen und etwas über sich erzählen können. Zu sehen sind die Ergebnisse unter anderem auf Messen in ganz Europa.

In the third dimension, brands have the chance to show more than their name and logo: their personality, the world they are at home in and what they stand for.

We think, feel and act 360° degrees. We work holistically and interdisciplinarily. Translating attention-grabbing ideas into corporate architecture if required. This allows us to create experiences in space that give brands a special radiance which inspire trust, because they promote strong identification and long-term loyalty, giving brands a sustainable stage so that they shine and tell something about themselves. The results can be seen at trade fairs throughout Europe.

MILEI - FOOD INGREDIENTS EUROPE, PARIS 2019

Für das Leutkirchener Unternehmen MILEI gilt es ein neues Messestand-Konzept zu entwickeln. Ziel ist es, dessen Produktwelt aus Milch und Molke zu visualisieren und erlebbar zu machen. Dazu übertragen wir die Formensprache des Logos dreidimensional in den Messestand. Runde Sitznischen zitieren die in der Milchlagerung verwendeten Edelstahlgefäße, die zu Cocooning-Zwecken flexibel geschlossen werden können. Deckenwellen symbolisieren den Fluss von Milch. Und die Theke nimmt die Form eines Tropfens und Eiswagens auf. Das Farbenspiel der Logo- und Produktfarben findet sich in der fließenden Illuminierung des Messestands wieder und lädt den ebenfalls von uns entwickelten Claim „Live. Love. Enjoy" emotional auf.

MILEI - FOOD INGREDIENTS EUROPE, PARIS 2019

A new trade fair stand concept had to be developed for the Leutkirchen-based company MILEI. The aim is to visualise and bring to life the product world of milk and whey. For this purpose, we transferred the formal language of the logo three-dimensionally into the trade fair stand. Round seating niches quote the stainless used in milk storage, which can be closed flexibly for cocooning purposes. Ceiling waves symbolise the flow of milk and the counter takes on the shape of a drip and ice cream cart. The play of colours of the logo and product is reflected in the illumination of the exhibition stand, also developed by us. Love and enjoy.

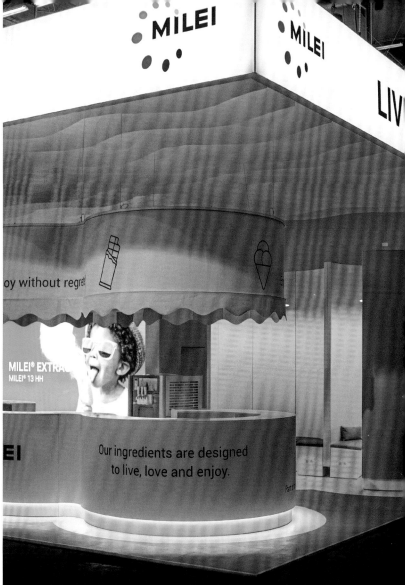

KÄSSBOHRER - INTERALPIN INNSBRUCK, 2017

Auf zwei Ebenen und einer Fläche von 1.000 qm möchten wir die technischen Vorzüge der leistungsstarken Pistenraupen präsentieren und zugleich der Marke PistenBully Leben einhauchen. Dazu erschaffen wir eine Welt, welche die PistenBully eindrucksvoll in ihrem natürlichen Habitat zeigt: steil am schneebedeckten Berghang. Im Gegensatz dazu spiegelt sich die gemütliche Atmosphäre der Berghütten in den in warmen Holztönen gehaltenen Gesprächsbereichen wider. Die besondere statische Herausforderung: Da sich unter der Messehalle eine Tiefgarage befindet, gilt es das Gewicht der jeweils 12 Tonnen wiegenden Fahrzeuge exakt zu verteilen.

KÄSSBOHRER - INTERALPIN INNSBRUCK, 2017

On two levels and an area of 1.000 m², we would like to present the technical advantages of the powerful snow groomers and at the same time breathe life into the PistenBully brand. To do this, we created a world that shows the PistenBully impressively in its natural habitat: steeply on a snow-covered mountain slope. In contrast, the cosy atmosphere of the mountain huts is reflected in the conversation areas, which are decorated in warm wood tones. An special static challenge: since there is an underground car park under the exhibition hall, the weight of the vehicles, each weighing 12 tons, must be distributed exactly.

REFERENZ CARADO - CARAVAN SALON DÜSSELDORF 2019

Wir entwerfen ein modulares und skalierbares Konzept, das international auf Reisemessen adaptiert wird. Die Symbolik und Form des Carado-Logos ist Grundlage für eine emotionale Aufladung der Markenwerte. „Sonne" und „Wasser" finden sich an prominenten Stellen wieder. Etwa als orangen strahlender Halbkreis, der – gemeinsam mit Leuchtelementen der gleichen Farbe – auf den Urlaub einstimmt. Die Fahrzeuge reihen sich sternförmig um die Infotheke, die als eine Art Marktplatz zentral angelegt ist. „Wasser" wird mit einem 12 Meter großen Logo-Element mit bespielbarer LED-Fläche visualisiert. Der separate Bewirtungsbereich nutzt mit seinen Sitznischen den bestehenden Platz optimal. Atmosphärische Bigprints spielen mit der Reiselust der Messebesucher. Das markante Baukastensystem sorgt auf dem 1.200 qm großen Messestand für Wohlbefinden, Wiedererkennbarkeit und Orientierung.

REFERENCE CARADO - CARAVAN SALON DÜSSELDORF 2019

We designed a modular and scalable concept that can be adapted internationally for travel fairs. The symbolism and form of the Carado logo is the basis for an emotional charging of the brand values. "Sonne" and "Wasser" can be found in prominent places. For example, in the form of a radiant orange semicircle that, together with lighting elements of the same colour, creates a holiday mood. The vehicles are lined up in a star shape around the information counter, which is centrally located as a kind of marketplace. "Wasser" is visualised by a 12 m. logo element with a playable LED surface. The separate catering area with its seating niches makes optimum use of the existing space. Atmospheric bigprints play with the fair visitors' desire to travel. The striking modular system ensures well-being, recognition and orientation on the 1.200 m² of stand.

carado

HIER GIBT'S URLAUBSGELD!

WÄHREND UNSERER MESSEAKTION GEBEN WIR IHNEN EINEN SATTEN
PREISNACHLASS AUF IHR WUNSCHFAHRZEUG. DA BLEIBT VIEL GELD FÜR
IHRE URLAUBSKASSE ÜBRIG.

MESSE-
AKTION!

SICHERN SIE SICH
IHREN PREISVORTEIL!

VLOWING
STATT NUR CAMPEN.

made in
GERMANY

REFERENZ WINTERHALTER - HOST MILANO 2019

Die Anforderungen im übergeordneten Messekonzept Winterhalters sind präzise umrissen. In der Gestaltung sollen Klarheit, Orientierung und Produktinszenierung deutlich zum Tragen kommen. Unsere Lösung: Mittels Leuchtenbanner fassen wir den Messebereich selbstbewusst ein, um bereits von Weitem eine gute Wiedererkennbarkeit und Markendifferenzierung zu garantieren. Quadratische Leuchtelemente unterstützen die strenge Struktur, während Produktinseln für eine stilsichere Präsentation der gewerblichen Spülmaschinen sorgen. In kontrastreicher Kombination von kühler Unternehmensfarbe mit dem natürlichen Material Holz schaffen wir eine Atmosphäre, die Besucher zum Bleiben und Wohlfühlen einlädt.

REFERENCE WINTERHALTER - HOST MILANO 2019

The requirements in Winterhalter's trade fair concept are precisely outlined. In the design, clarity, orientation and product staging should be clearly expressed. Our solution: we confidently surround the trade fair area to guarantee good recognition and brand differentiation even from a distance. Square lighting elements support the austere structure, while product islands ensure a stylish presentation of the commercial dishwashers. In a high-contrast combination of cool corporate colour with the natural material wood, we create an atmosphere that invites visitors to stay and feel good.

STUDIO LAKRITS

Michaela Brunner & Jvo Ruppanner

Oft — ach was, meist zielen wir direkt auf das Herz oder den Bauch. Dahin, wo die grossen Emotionen sitzen. Wofür sonst lohnt es sich, Bühnen zu erschaffen? Geboren ist diese Haltung aus der Leidenschaft für Kreativität und Konsequenz. Wir paaren sie mit gestalterischer Kompetenz und dem charakteristischen Anspruch an überzeugende Resultate, bei denen der Mensch mit seinen fünf Sinnen im Mittelpunkt steht. Dass wir dabei auch mal polarisieren, nehmen wir in Kauf. Eine Eventagentur sind wir nicht. Vielmehr Passionierte, die Kommunikation und szenische Architektur in einem harmonischen — und zielgerichteten — Ganzen aufgehen lassen. Dabei denken und handeln wir nachhaltig und verantwortungsbewusst. Und: Wir lassen uns immer gern herausfordern.

Often - oh what, mostly we aim directly at the heart or the stomach. That's where the big emotions are. What else is there to create stages for? This attitude is born from a passion for creativity and consistency. We combine it with creative competence and the characteristic demand for convincing results, in which the human being with his five senses is at the centre. We accept the fact that we sometimes polarise in the process. We are not an event agency. Rather, we are passionate about making communication and scenic architecture merge into a harmonious - and goal-oriented - whole. We think and act sustainably and responsibly. And: we always like to be challenged.

ALLIANZ CINEMA ZURICH

"Mut heisst, im Leben selbst Regie führen." Vor dem Hintergrund dieses Claims wurde der Allianz Cinema-Auftritt in den Städten Genf, Zürich und Basel konzipiert und mit Aktivitäten wie dem Mut-Rad gestaltet. In Zürich und Genf wurde als weitere Attraktion auch eine Photo Booth integriert.

CINEMA ZURICH ALLIANCE

"Courage means directing your own life". It was against this background that the Allianz Cinema presence in the cities of Geneva, Zurich and Basel was conceived and designed with activities such as the Courage Wheel. In Zurich and Geneva a Photo Booth was also integrated as a further attraction.

APPENZELLER SCHAUKÄSEREI

Arbeiten in einer geschichtsträchtigen Institution. Im Auftrag von und zusammen mit Curious About haben wir den am Ende seiner Reifezeit stehenden Schaubereich neu gestaltet und erlebbar gemacht. Heute werden Gäste durch den Shop/Marktplatz in den Erlebnisbereich gelotst, um mit einem Schlüssel in der Hand das Geheimnis des Käses zu erkunden und wissenswertes über den sorgfältigen Herstellungsprozess dieser lokalen Spezialität zu verinnerlichen.

APPENZELL SHOW DAIRY

Working in an institution steeped in history. On behalf of and together with Curious About, we have redesigned and brought to life the show area which is at the end of its maturity period. Today, guests are guided through the shop/marketplace to the experience area, where, with a key in their hand, they can explore the secret of the cheese and learn interesting facts about the careful production process of this local speciality.

TBWA \ ZÜRICH

3D-Konzept und Umsetzung des neuen Corporate Design für TBWA \ Zürich The Disruption© Company. Der frische — in Cannes mit dem bronzenen Löwen ausgezeichnete — Auftritt ist selbstbewusst und unterstreicht den disruptiven Charakter der Agentur. Wir haben das Konzept spezifisch für die Firmenräume konzipiert und es vor Ort umgesetzt. Wichtig war uns, dass der markante neue Auftritt mit der bestehenden Architektur harmonisiert und diese nicht belastet.

TBWA \ ZURICH

3D concept and implementation of the new corporate design for TBWA \ Zurich The Disruption© Company. The fresh appearance - awarded the bronze lion in Cannes - is self confident and underlines the agency's disruptive character. We designed the concept specifically for the company's premises and implemented it on site. It was important to us that the striking new appearance harmonizes with the existing architecture and does not burden it.

ZFV AN DER SWISS SKILLS

Fachkräftemangel ist neben vielen anderen Branchen auch in der Gastronomie ein Problem. Die Schweizer ZFV-Gastronomiegruppe möchte mit ihrem Auftritt den jungen Nachwuchs für sich gewinnen. Unser Konzept, ein schlichter, klar strukturierter Messestand mit unterschiedlichen „Karrierewegen" unterstützt dieses wichtige Unternehmensziel.

ZFV AT SWISS SKILLS

The lack of skilled workers is a problem in the catering industry as well as in many other sectors. The Swiss ZFV gastronomy group would like to win over young up-and-coming talent with its presentation. Our concept, a simple, clearly structured exhibition with different career paths supports this important corporate goal.

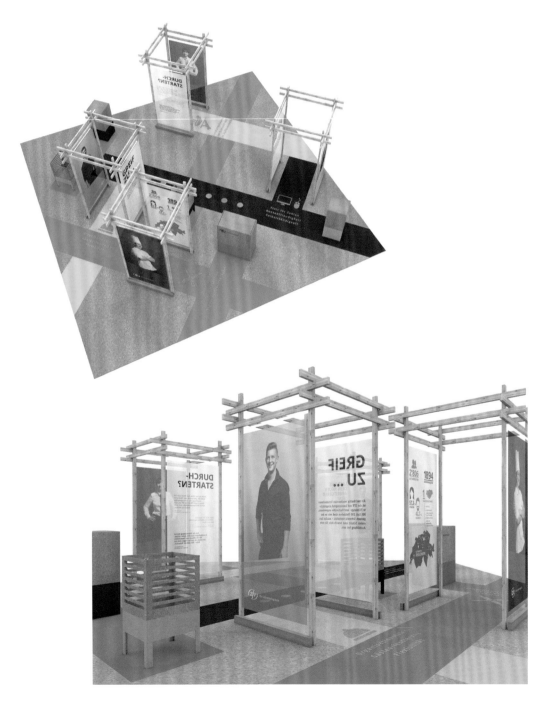

STUDIO SASCH

Alexander Hamm & Carlo Faust

Basierend auf dem Konzept eines Studios, in dem kreatives Design durch Austausch und Experiment stattfindet, verstehen wir uns als zukunftsorientierte Plattform für interdisziplinäre Interventionen zwischen Design und Architektur. Dieser Synergie-effekt spiegelt sich in nachhaltigen und ganzheitlichen Konzepten, die wir gemeinsam mit unseren Kunden entwickeln. STUDIO SASCH teilt mit Begeisterung ein offenes Interesse an Innovation und möchte einzigartige Möglichkeiten schaffen eine Form- und Materialsprache zu entwickeln, die dazu beiträgt Architektur erfahrbar zu machen. Im Spannungsfeld zwischen Architektur- Design- und Markenrepräsentation entstehen individuelle Projekte. Sie verstehen sich als spezifische Reaktion auf das kontextuelle Umfeld und zielen darauf ab das maximale Potential für seine NutzerInnen zu entfalten. Die Leidenschaft für puristisches Design und Innovation sind dabei ständiger Impulsgeber und Motivator unseres Teams.

Based on the concept of a studio where creative design takes place through exchange and experiment, we see ourselves as a future-oriented platform for interdisciplinary interventions between design and architecture. This synergy effect is reflected in sustainable and holistic concepts that we develop together with our clients. STUDIO SASCH enthusiastically shares an open interest in innovation and strives to develop a form and material language that contributes to making architecture tangible. Individual projects are created in the area of conflict between architecture, design, and brand representation. They see themselves as a specific reaction to the contextual environment and aim to develop the maximum potential for their users. The passion for purist design and innovation is a constant source of inspiration and motivation for our team.

DJI @ IFA (INTERNATIONALE FUNKAUSSTELLUNG) 2019, BERLIN

In Zusammenarbeit mit der Digitalagentur „HERREN DER SCHÖPFUNG" entstand anlässlich der IFA Berlin 2019 ein innovatives Messe- uns Kommunikationskonzept. Gemeinsam entwickelte man einen Ausstellungsraum zur Präsentation neuer Drohnen- und Bildstabilisierungsprodukte der Marke DJI. Ausgangspunkt für die Gestaltung sind große Bewegtbildflächen, welche sich an den gängigen digitalen Bildformaten (Landscape & Portrait) orientieren. Atemberaubende Drohnenaufnahmen entfalten das Produktpotential auf den LED Screens, die gleichzeitig als strukturierende Elemente der Ausstellungsfläche dienen. Als Schlüsselelement des Stands lädt der „Flight Cage" die BesucherInnen zur aktiven Partizipation ein. Durch das interaktive Produkterlebnis wird eine Lebendigkeit erzeugt, die den Ausstellungsraum in eine Erlebniswelt wandelt. Die gro.zügige Flächenbespielung und offene Architektur ermöglichen einen direkten Zugang zur Standfläche. Im Zentrum stehen Ausstellungstische, die den Fokus ganz uneingeschränkt auf das Produkt lenken. Das Designkonzept integriert eine anspruchsvolle interaktive Mediatektur und kombiniert eine klare Formensprache mit rationalem Design.

DJI @ IFA (INTERNATIONAL CONSUMER ELECTRONICS FAIR) 2019, BERLIN

In cooperation with the digital agency "HERREN DER SCHÖPFUNG", an innovative trade fair and communication concept was developed for the IFA Berlin 2019. We created a showroom for the presentation of DJI's new drone and image stabilisation products. The design consists of moving image surfaces based on the common digital image formats (landscape and portrait). Breathtaking drone images unfold the product potential on LED screens, which also serve as structural elements for the exhibition space. As a focal element of the stand, the "Flight Cage" invites visitors to actively participate. The interactive product experience creates a liveliness that transforms the exhibition space into an experiential world. The generous use of space and open architecture allow direct access to the stand area. Exhibition tables focusing entirely on the product are displayed at the centre. The design concept integrates a sophisticated interactive mediatecture and combines a clear formal language with rational design.

HYUNDAI IONIQ ROADSHOW 2016

In Form einer Roadshow präsentierte Hyundai IONIQ 2016 fortschrittliche Technologien zum Thema Elektromobilität in europäischen Großstädten. Im öffentlichen Raum fungierte der Ausstellungspavillon als Informationszentrum für Mobilitätsbedürfnisse und Nachhaltigkeit. Die transparente Fassade und rundum Zugänglichkeit lassen den Pavillon mit dem pulsierenden Leben des Stadtraums verschmelzen. Als verantwortliche Projektmanager Space & Design entwickelten wir für unsren Kunden INNOCEAN Worldwide Europe (Lead Agentur), gemeinsam mit unseren Partnern MUTABOR (Architektur) und HERREN DER SCHÖPFUNG (Exponate) einen visionäres Konzept, das wir in den Städten Amsterdam, Mailand, Oslo und Frankfurt präsentieren durften. Symbolisch für den Informationsfluss wurde ein Wasserkreislaufs angelegt, der die kreisförmige Architektursprache widerspiegelt. Der offene und einladende Charakter bildet eine Plattform für Austausch und Vision. Unterstützend wirkt sich die dynamische Formgebung auf die Anforderungen des Zeigens, Erlebens und Mitgestaltens aus. Als visuelles Herzstück der Ausstellung nimmt eine interaktive Wandinstallation die Zukunftswünsche der Passanten auf und inszeniert diese per Video Tracking als Wasserfall. Mit dem zentralen Interaktionselement konnten Ideen gesammelt und anschließend auf sozialen Netzwerken geteilt werden.

HYUNDAI IONIQ ROADSHOW 2016

In the form of a roadshow, Hyundai IONIQ 2016 presented advanced technologies on the subject of electromobility in European cities. In a public space, the exhibition pavilion served as an information centre for mobility needs and sustainability. The transparent façade and all-round accessibility allowed the pavilion to merge with the electric life of the urban space. As the responsible project manager Space & Design we developed for our customer INNOCEAN Worldwide Europe (Lead agency), together with our partners MUTABOR (architecture) and HERREN DER SCHÖPFUNG (Exhibits) a visionary concept which we were able to present in the cities of Amsterdam, Milan, Oslo, and Frankfurt. A water circuit symbolising the flow of information was expressed through a circle-themed architectural language whose open and inviting character forms a platform for exchange and vision. The dynamic design supports the requirements of showing, experiencing, and participating in the design. As the visual heart of the exhibition, an interactive wall installation processes the passers-by's future wishes and displays them as a waterfall via video tracking. With the central interaction element, ideas could be collected and shared on social media.

UEBERHOLZ

Nico Ueberholz

Ueberholz ist Agentur und Werkstatt, ist Sparringspartner, Ideengeber. Antreiber und Umsetzer. Die vom Geschäftsführer Nico Ueberholz 1986 gründete vielfach ausgezeichnete Designagentur arbeitet im internationalen Bereich. Sie ist Partner für Kunden aus unterschiedlichen Fachbereichen: Aus Industrie, Wirtschaft, Verbänden und Kultur. Für Viele arbeiten sie schon Jahre lang. Immer wie neu und zukunftsorientiert auf der Suche, nach passenden Formaten und Lösungen für Ausstellungen, Roadshows, Corporate Designs, Messeauftritte, Shops, Exponate, Veranstaltungen, Licht und Produkte. Ein kommunikatives und kreatives interdisziplinäres Team begleitet die Kunden vom Entwurf bis zur Umsetzung und Fertigstellung. Das ist effizientes Arbeiten ohne Overheads. Das 2014 selbst konzipierte und gebaute Office in Wuppertal ist die 3D Visitenkarte des Unternehmens. Hier wird sichtbar, wofür der Name Ueberholz steht. Klarheit. Material. Überraschend anders. Ueberholz Office, das sind 600 qm Freiraum für Kreativität, Leidenschaft und Vision.

Ueberholz is an agency and workshop, is a sparring partner, a source of ideas. Drivers and converters. The design agency, which was founded in 1986 by the managing director Nico Ueberholz, has won many awards and works in the international field. It is a partner for customers from various specialist areas: from industry, business, associations and culture. They have been working for many for years. Always looking like new and future-oriented, looking for suitable formats and solutions for exhibitions, road shows, corporate designs, trade fair appearances, shops, exhibits, events, lighting and products. A communicative and creative interdisciplinary team accompanies customers from design to implementation and completion. That is efficient work without overheads. The office in Wuppertal, designed and built in 2014, is the company's 3D business card. Here you can see what the name Ueberholz stands for. Clarity. Material. Surprisingly different. Ueberholz Office, that's 600 square meters of space for creativity, passion and vision.

LICHTZEITRAUM - TEILNAHME AN DER ARCHITEKTUR BIENALE VENEDIG 2016

Licht formt Raum und macht diesen als Raum in unterschiedlichen Formen mehrdimensional erlebbar. Der Licht-zeitRaum ist eine Licht-in Raum-Installation von Ueberholz auf der Architektur-Biennale in Venedig. Pulsierendes Licht im Takt sonorer Herzschlagtöne, formt auf 15 qm Metern unterschiedliche Raum-in Raum Erlebnisse. In kurzer zeitlicher Abfolge wechseln Enge und Weite, Höhe und Tiefe in ein und demselben Raum. Der Blick durch ein virtu-elles Fenster auf den Canale Grande passt sich der jeweiligen Raum-Inszenierung an. Licht beeinflusst kommunikati-ve Prozesse. Die Biennale-Installation basiert auf der Idee, Licht als schöpferische Kraft für architektonische Räume in all ihrer emotionalen Vielfalt und zeitlichen Begrenztheit erfahrbar zu machen.

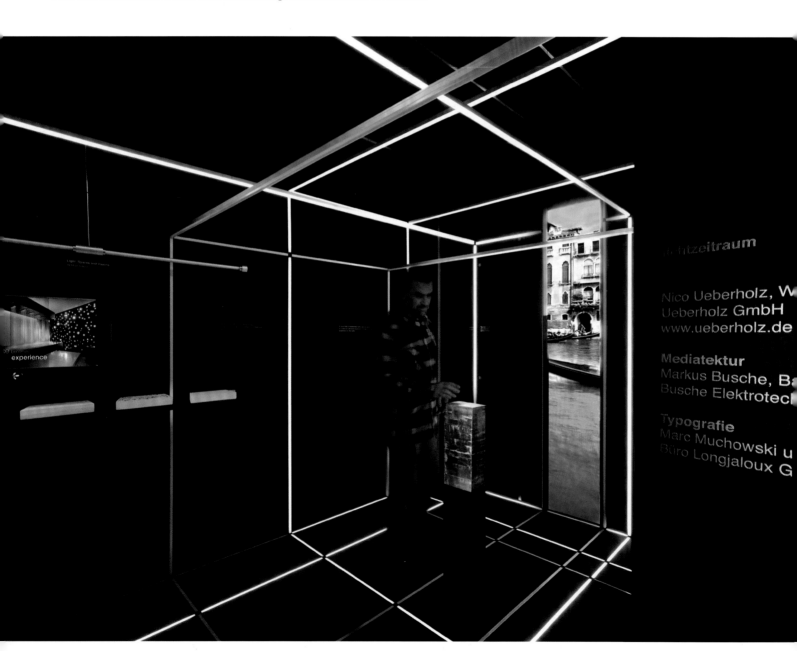

experience

itzeitraum

Nico Ueberholz, W
Ueberholz GmbH
www.ueberholz.de

Mediatektur
Markus Busche, B
Busche Elektrotech

Typografie
Marc Muchowski u
Büro Longjaloux G

LICHTZEITRAUM - PARTICIPATION IN THE ARCHITECTURE BIENALE VENICE 2016

Light shapes space and allows it to be experienced as space in different shapes. The LichtzeitRaum is a light-in-space installation by Ueberholz at the Architecture Biennale in Venice. Pulsating light in the rhythm of sonorous heartbeat tones, forms different room-in-room experiences on 15 square meters. In a short time sequence, narrow and wide, height and depth alternate in one and the same room. The view through a virtual window onto the Canale Grande adapts to the respective room setting. Light influences communicative processes. The Biennale installation is based on the idea of making light as a creative force for architectural spaces tangible in all its emotional diversity and temporal limitation.

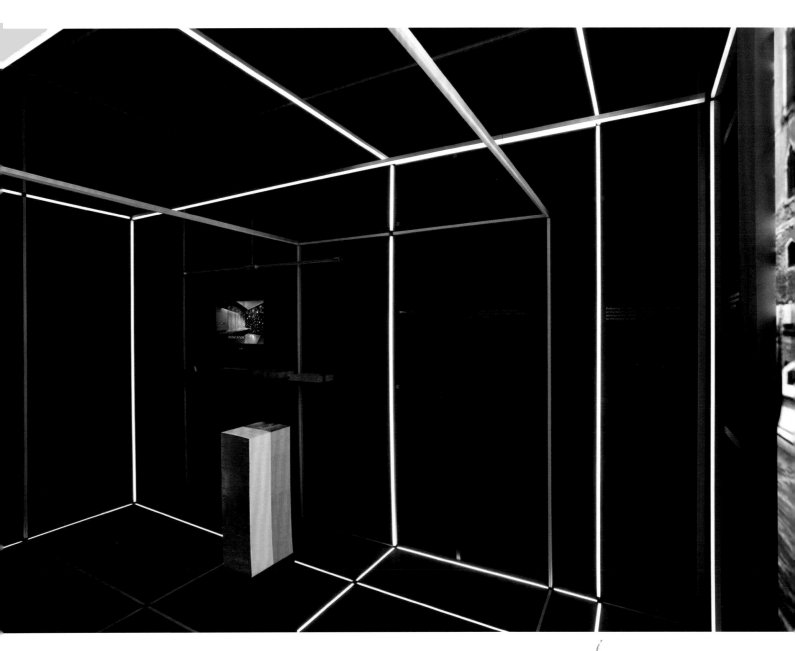

AMTICO, BAU 2019 IN MÜNCHEN

Amtico makes it possible – eine konsequente Vielfalt in jeder Dimension. So lässt sich das Standkonzept von Amtico auf der Bau 2019 in München perfekt beschreiben. Für den Hersteller von hochwertigen Bodenbelegen, in außergewöhnlich in Farbe und Muster, inszeniert Ueberholz einzelne verspiegelte Räume, die aus einfachem, unbehandeltem Sperrholz bestehen. Sie zeigen durch den Einsatz von Spiegelflächen, die unendliche Produktvielfalt und deren Kombinationsmöglichkeiten. Diese dreidimensionalen Produkträume verbinden so den analogen und digitalen Markenraum. 104 qm Messeauftritt, die Akzente setzen und den Raum zum Blickfang werden lassen. Das Motto des Herstellers Amtico „A splash of colour. Mach das Leben bunt und lebendig" wird hier bis die letzte Ecke des Standkonzeptes umgesetzt.

AMTICO, BAU 2019 IN MUNICH

Amtico makes it possible - consistent diversity in every dimension. This is how Amtico's stand concept at Bau 2019 in Munich can be perfectly described. For the manufacturer of high-quality floor coverings, in unusual colors and patterns, Ueberholz stages individual mirrored rooms made of simple, untreated plywood. Through the use of mirror surfaces, they show the infinite variety of products and their possible combinations. These three-dimensional product spaces thus connect the analog and digital brand space. 104 sqm trade fair appearance that set accents and make the room an eye-catcher. The motto of the manufacturer Amtico "A splash of color. Make life colorful and lively" is implemented here down to the last corner of the stand concept.

MERTENS, AMBIENTE 2019 IN FRANKFURT

Für die traditionelle Besteck- und Messer-Manufaktur Mertens, die 2019 ihr hundertjähriges Bestehen feiert, erstellt Ueberholz zur Ambiente einen Messestand mit viel Liebe zum Detail und hoher Qualität. Highlight hier ist der Entwurf von passenden Präsentations- und Kommunikationsmöbeln zur bestehenden historischen Werkbank. Der raw belassene Hallenboden unterstreicht den Handwerkscharakter. Kochen und genießen im stylischen Ambiente. Hier können sich Besucher auf den 33 Quadratmetern auf die Reise machen, schöne Lifestyle- Produkte zu entdecken, um dann an dem langen werkbankartigen Arbeitstisch zu einem Gespräch zusammenzukommen.

MERTENS, AMBIENCE 2019 IN FRANKFURT

For the traditional cutlery and knife manufacturer Mertens, which is celebrating its centenary in 2019, Ueberholz is creating an exhibition stand for Ambiente with great attention to detail and high quality. The highlight here is the design of suitable presentation and communication furniture for the existing historical workbench. The raw hall floor underscores the craftsmanship. Cook and enjoy in a stylish ambience. Here visitors can set out on a journey of 33 square meters, discover beautiful lifestyle products, and then come together for a conversation at the long workbench-like work table.

ANDREAS FUHRIMANN
GABRIELLE HÄCHLER

ARCHITEKTEN ETH BSA SIA AG
Hardturmstrasse 66
CH-8005 Zürich
T +41 44 271 04 80
mail@afgh.ch
www.afgh.ch

ATELIER BRÜCKNER GMBH
Krefelder Straße 32
70376 Stuttgart
T +49 711 50 00 770
F +49 711 50 00 7722
atb@atelier-brueckner.com
www.atelier-brueckner.com
Photos: © Atelier Brückner, Michael-Reiner,
Marcus Sies, Michael Jungblut

ATELIER MARKGRAPH
Mainzer Landstraße 193
60326 Frankfurt am Main
T +49 69 97993 0
F +49 69 97993 1181
contact@markgraph.de
www.markgraph.de
Photos: © Kristof Lemp, Andreas Keller

BRANDHERM + KRUMREY
INTERIOR ARCHITECTURE

Schanzenstraße 27
51063 Köln
T +49 221 9321036
koeln@b-k-i.de

Donnerstraße 20
22763 Hamburg
T +49 40 65044650
hamburg@b-k-i.de
www.b-k-i.de
Photos: © Joachim Grothus

CBA CLEMENS BACHMANN ARCHITEKTEN
Hans-Preißinger-Str. 8, Gebäude C
81379 München
T +49 89 2300070 18
F +49 89 2300070 29
office@cbarchitekten.com
www.cbarchitekten.com
Photos: © CBA Clemens Bachmann
Architekten

COPYRIGHT COMMUNICATIONS GMBH
Speicherstr. 59
60327 Frankfurt am Main
T +49 69 34 87 6650
F +49 69 34 87 66599
info@copyrightcommunications.de
www.copyrightcommunications.de
Photos: © Florian Trettenbach,
Copyright Communications

DAYDREAMERS DESIGN
8A, Sing Kui Commercial Building
27 des Voeux Road West, Sheung Wan
Hong Kong
T +852 5110 7950
studio@daydreamersdesign.hk
www.daydreamersdesign.hk
Photos: © daydreamers

DESIGNBÜRO FÖN, DESIGN_
DIPL. ING. FH FB INNENARCHITEKTUR
ARKAS FÖRSTNER
Oberndorfer Straße 5
78713 Schramberg
T +49 7422 520 351
info@foen-design.com
www.foendesign.com
Photos: © Matthias Hangst, Olaf Schiemann,
Arkas Förstner

DIPL. ING. WERNER R. QUADT
INNENARCHTEKT AKNW I BDIA
BERRENRATHER STR. 188 A
50937 KÖLN
T +49 221 9439690
F +49 221 9439691
werner.quadt@quadt-koeln.de
www.quadt-koeln.de
Photos: © Stefanie Heublein

GIGLER HOLZ-DESIGN
Winkl 2
83115 Neubeuern
T +49 8035 963 908 0
info@holz-design-gigler.de
www.holz-design-gigler.de
Photos: © GIGLER holz-design

JOCHEN HUNGER MUSEUM &
EXHIBITION DESIGN
Gerberei 19
91054 Erlangen
T +49 09131 8299791
jh@jochenhunger.com
www.jochenhunger.com
Photos: © Daniel Schäfer

JÜRGENSARCHITEKTEN
Thierschstraße 12
80538 München
T +49 89 21 550 6580
info@juergensarchitekten.de
www.juergensarchitekten.de
Photos: © Tobias Vollmer, Sandra Schuck,
3S Frankenmöbel und kbw brands

KAUFFMANN THEILIG & PARTNER
FREIE ARCHITEKTEN BDA
Zeppelinstraße 10
73760 Ostfildern
T +49 711 4 51 22 0
F +49 711 4 51 22 40
info@ktp-architekten.de
www.ktp-architekten.de
Photos: © Andreas Keller, Markus Bollen

LAUFEN BATHROOMS AG
Wahlenstrasse 46
CH-4242 Laufen
T +41 61 765 71 11
feedback@laufen.ch
www.laufen.ch

Photos: © Andri Pol, Eleonora Rapacchietta,
Max Zambelli, Oliver Helbig, Joel Cartier,
Ilco Kemmere, Laufen AG

MAIER + HOLLENBECK ARCHITEKTEN
Regentenstr. 42
51063 Köln
T +49 221 2714170
F +49 221 27141729
info@maier-hollenbeck.de
www.maier-hollenbeck.de
Photos: © Patrick Schwarz, Axel Hartmann,
Peter Hinschläger

PRINZTRÄGER
LARISSA PRINZ & MARIE TRÄGER GBR
HEDWIGSTR. 5
44809 BOCHUM
T +49 234 95717311
post@prinztraeger.de
www.prinztraeger.de
Photos: © Bande für Gestaltung

RANGER DESIGN
Franklinstraße 3
70435 Stuttgart
T +49 711 99 31 630
F +49 711 99 31 6333
contact@ranger-design.com
www.ranger-design.com
Photos: © Ranger Design

RAUMKONTOR INNENARCHITEKTUR
Oberrather Str. 12
40472 Düsseldorf
T 0211 48 69 67
F 0211 48 62 30
www.raumkontor.com
kontakt@raumkontor.com
Photos: © Hans Jürgen Landes,
bildhübsche fotografie, Andreas Körner

SONS GMBH
Zwingerstraße 2
87435 Kempten
T +49 831 512360
sons@go-sons.de
www.go-sons.de
Photos: © Sons GmbH

STUDIO LAKRITS
szenische architektur + design
Gotthardstrasse 62
CH - 8800 Thalwil
T +41 44 204 38 00
info@lakrits.ch
www.lakrits.ch
Photos: © Christoph Eugster, Jerry Gross,
Michaela Brunner, Andrea Camen

STUDIO SASCH
Hanauer Landstrasse 192
60314 Frankfurt am Main
T +49 692 073 5351
info@studiosasch.de
www.studiosasch.de
Photos: © Carlo Faust, Cem Yücetas

UEBERHOLZ GMBH
Vorm Eichholz 2e
42119 Wuppertal
T +49 202 280 960
F +49 202 280 9666
info@ueberholz.de
www.ueberholz.de
Photos: © Ulrich Beuttenmüller,
Olaf Becker-Lacorn

KECK
KECK
MANUFACTURER OF THE ORIGINAL
INFLATABLE EVENT TENT
X-GLOO
Tents for Events
KECK
KECK

KECK

KE

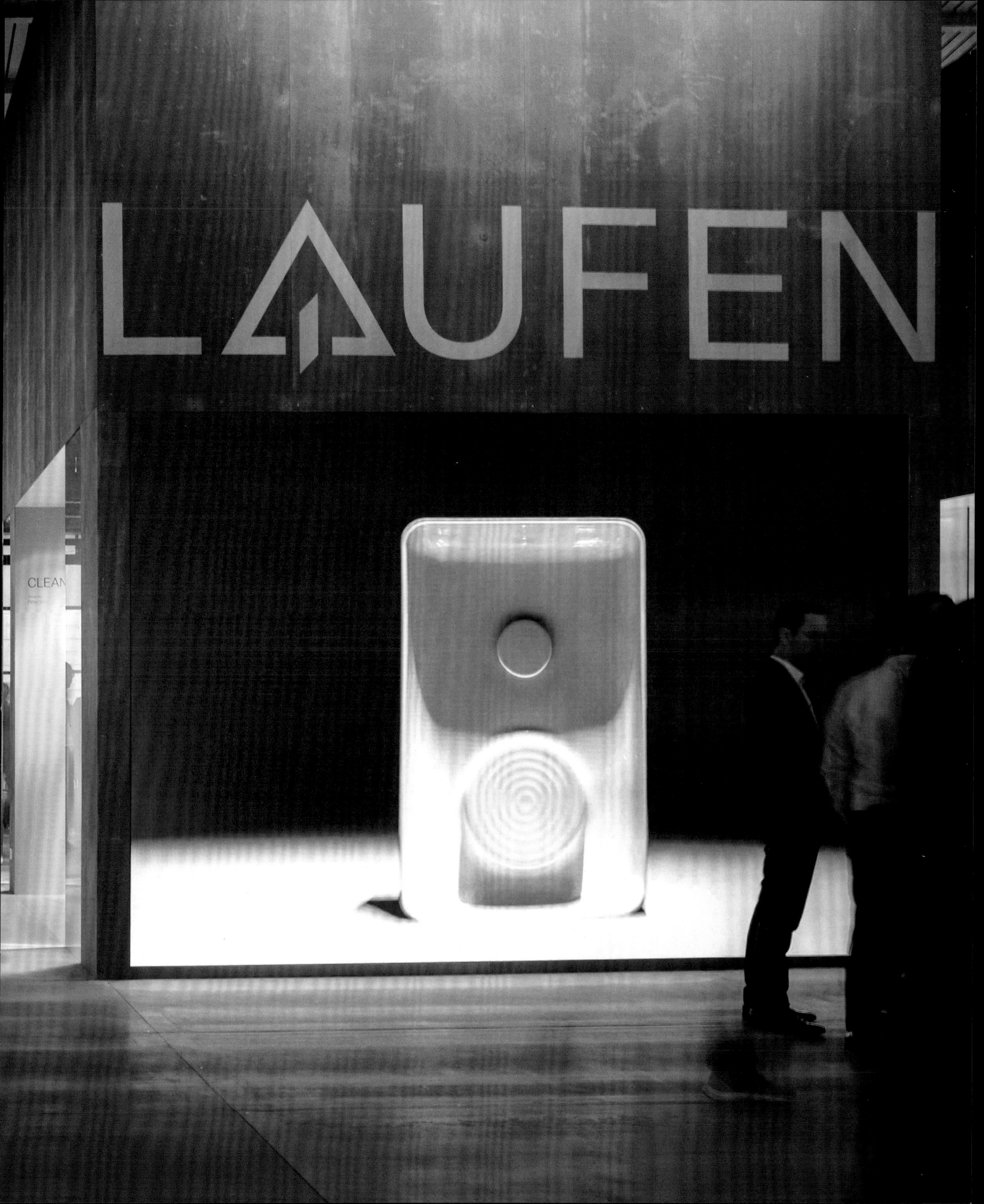
LAUFEN
CLEAN

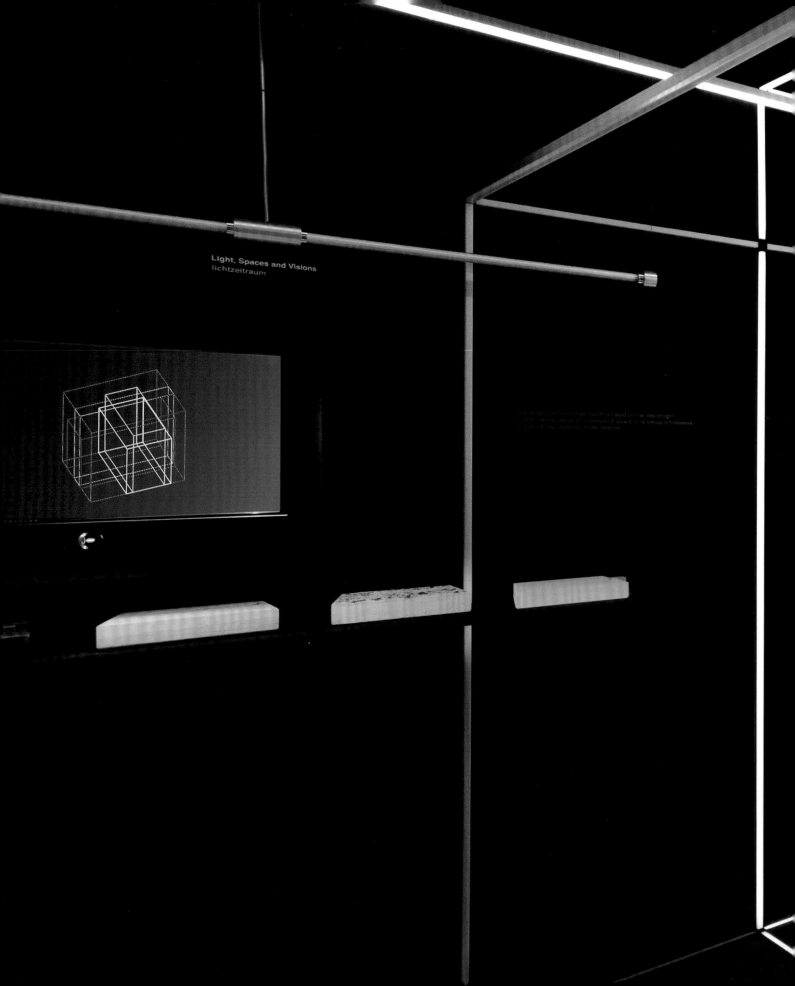

Light, Spaces and Visions
lichtzeitraum